Everything
you always wanted
your babysitter to know

Linda Doeser

PIATKUS

© 1981 Linda Doeser

First published in 1981 by Judy Piatkus
(Publishers) Limited of Loughton, Essex

Doeser, Linda
  Everything you always wanted
  your babysitter to know.
  1. Children – care and hygiene
  2. Babysitters
  I. Title
  649'.1'0248   HQ769

ISBN 0-86188-109-5

Designed by Paul Saunders
Cover illustrated by Camron Design

Typeset by V & M Graphics Ltd, Aylesbury, Bucks
Printed and bound by R. J. Acford, Chichester

Contents

Everything you always
wanted your babysitter to know

Introduction

Being a parent should not make you a prisoner serving a ten-
or twelve-year sentence in your own home. Yet many people
are reluctant to leave their children in someone else's care.
This need no longer be a problem. With the aid of this book,
you can choose a babysitter with confidence and leave her
fully in charge and able to cope with any contingency.

Check-lists throughout the book ensure that you need
never again rush to the telephone halfway through dinner
because you forgot to say where the clean nappies are kept.

Easy-to-follow instructions, from bottle-feeding a baby to
coping with a ten-year-old's nightmares, provide even the
most inexperienced babysitter with all the help she needs.
Separate sections of the book deal with children of different
ages, looking after them both inside and outside the house.

How to use this book

Check-lists and information sheets are included at the ends of
their relevant chapters. Fill them in, or prepare your own
lists, before you go out, selecting the details that refer to your
children. Your babysitter will then have all the information
she needs at her fingertips and in one place. It is advisable to
use pencil so that the information can be updated as the
children grow older or as circumstances change.

A note on the sexes

For convenience, the pronouns 'he' and 'him' have been used
to refer to the children. Babysitters, on the other hand,
have been referred to as 'she'.

PART ONE

1

Assessing Your Needs

All kinds of people are willing, at one time or another, to act as babysitters. They range from the lady who lives next door and has three children of her own to the local schoolgirl saving money to go pony trekking next summer. However, trusting the safety and welfare of your precious offspring to the tender mercies of a stranger is not undertaken lightly, and it is not the same thing as employing someone to do the housework, for example. So how do you go about finding that ideal – a babysitter whom you can trust, who is responsible and whom the children genuinely like?

The answer is, first, to assess honestly and truthfully your exact needs. The mother of two active schoolchildren needs a different person from the mother of one very small baby. A recalcitrant eight-year-old will pay far more attention to someone of his mother's generation than he will to a teenager barely ten years his senior.

How often and for how long?

If you are planning to return to work, or you are an active member of a voluntary aid association, or you try to visit an old or infirm parent every fortnight, then you need a babysitter on a regular basis and you need to be very business-like. Relying on a good-natured neighbour is not enough. You need to find someone with whom you can make a standing arrangement for every Tuesday, every other Thursday afternoon or whatever. You must be prepared to pay for her services or to offer a reciprocal service yourself (see Chapter 2, Getting the Right Person) and it is most important that you should stick to your side of the agreement as firmly as you expect her to stick to hers.

If you need a babysitter every day, then this is the time to consider 'professionals' — people who look after other people's children for a living, such as childminders and nursery nurses. You need to find one, really reliable and efficient person who will give continuity to your children's lives and you must treat her like the treasure she is.

For occasional babysitting, a number of different people is perfectly all right and may well be positively helpful, adding new interest and variety. 'Amateur' babysitters — neighbours, members of the family, friends and teenagers — are often willing to look after a child for a few hours once in a while, provided that they are not called upon too often and that they are given sufficient notice.

Another point to consider is the length of time for which you will need the babysitter. The 'amateurs' can all be relied upon to spare a few hours while you are at the theatre or at a dinner party, for example.

Prolonged care of children, even a whole day, can be very exhausting for people who are not used to it, and both babysitter and children can end up bad-tempered and thoroughly wretched. Once again, the 'professional' is worth considering. Although her services are almost always more expensive than the 'amateur's', she is efficient and trained to cope with all situations.

How many and how old?

The type of babysitter you require will also depend very much on the number of children she has to look after and on their ages. It hardly needs pointing out that one child is less work than two.

Grandparents, those great stalwarts of family organization, delight in every opportunity to see their grandchildren. However, it is many years since they had to cope with rumbustious toddlers, and entertaining the entire family is quite different from sole responsibility for its youngest members. This does not mean that grandparents should never be asked to babysit. On the contrary, as familiar and well-loved faces, they offer the children real security in their parents' absence. They are especially welcome babysitters if you have older children or a very young baby.

The all-purpose babysitter is probably the friend or neighbour who has children of her own. She is used to coping with the demands of a family. Changing nappies or bottle-feeding hold no terrors for her and she will not take any nonsense from eight-year-olds who refuse to go to bed. As a mother herself, she tends to have a more or less natural authority, which children are quick to recognize and respect.

Young people, perhaps the son or daughter of a friend, a girl guide, or a schoolgirl studying for 'A' levels, are usually very reliable and make up for their lack of experience in handling children with real enthusiasm and willingness. Nevertheless, they should never be given more responsibility than they can confidently handle. Caring for one child is usually quite enough for the inexperienced sitter and she is generally best left in charge of one who is expected to sleep throughout the duration of her duty. Young people often show surprising patience with toddlers and a great deal of ingenuity about the games and stories they invent to amuse their young charges.

However, they may become very flustered if they are expected to do much more than keep an eye on the child and perhaps amuse him for a short time. Ensure that tasks such as preparing tea are over before the teenage sitter arrives. At the very least, try to ensure that she does them while you are still there to lend a helping hand.

Older children will quickly detect uncertainty and lack of self-confidence in a babysitter and will press home the advantage with increasingly naughty behaviour. Teenagers are really too close in age to such children and it is unfair on both parties to expect them to manage. They simply do not have the authority that they feel they should have.

Night and day

The time of day when she will be required also affects your choice. Fortunately, most 'amateurs' are available in the evenings, the time when they are most often required.

However, some older people are very nervous about being alone late at night, especially in a strange house. Do check this before arranging to be out until 2 am. Also, if your babysitter has to be up early for school, her parents may be less than enthusiastic about her returning home in the early hours.

Finally, give a thought to transport home for the babysitter. If you have been out celebrating, you may not be able to drive her and, if it is very late at night, there may be no public transport. Once again, the ideal is a neighbour who has only to walk a few yards along the road. Another solution to the problem is to arrange for your sitter to stay overnight.

Daytime babysitting is much more difficult to arrange. If you need a daytime sitter for just one occasion, then the stalwart neighbour or friend may be able to help out, if she is available. The parents of your child's schoolfriend will often be willing to accept a temporary extra member of the family. This is a good solution, causing minimum disruption in the child's life and ensuring he is well looked after and happy.

If you are returning to work or need a babysitter for fairly frequent daytime care, then you should consider engaging the services of a 'professional'.

You may be able to arrange your working hours so that you are generally home before your children return from school. In this case, a wise mother plans an emergency service. It is best to make a standing arrangement with a neighbour or another parent, whom you can telephone when the need arises. A sensible and satisfactory way of organizing this is for you and her to agree to help each other out when necessary (see Chapter 2, Getting the Right Person). Also, explain to your child that, if you are not where he normally expects to see you, he should go to Mrs. Smith and to no one else.

Staying away from home

It may suit you better if your children stay with the babysitter rather than having her come to your home to look after them. The ideal person for this role is a grandparent, aunt or other tolerant relative, or the parents of another child, preferably a schoolfriend or chum of the same age. This will ensure that the child enjoys himself and is, therefore, much more likely to behave well. It also means that the house where he will be staying is familiar to him and/or organized to cope with playing buses in the hall, football in the garden, washing dolls' clothes in the bath or besieging a castle in the dining room. The homes of childless friends may not be so suitable.

Around the house

It is particularly important to be completely realistic about your needs if you are planning to employ one of the 'professionals' or to have someone actually living in your home, like an au pair. Any amount of bad feeling, temper and frustration can result from not making your requirements absolutely clear at the outset. Do you simply want someone to look after the children or do you expect help with the housework and shopping as well? If you are asking too much, it will quickly become apparent when you contact an agency or when no one replies to your advertisements. In this case, you need to think again, but this is much better than employing someone under false pretences and having a trained nanny (never cheap at the best of times) fuming over the washing-up or walking out in a huff because you gave her a basket of laundry. Equally, remember that a woman who is quite happy to do a couple of hours cleaning each morning, may not be willing or able to change nappies and heat up the ten o'clock feed. Decide exactly what you want and make your needs clear from the start.

The eleventh hour

Babysitters do not spend their entire lives at the end of a telephone waiting for you to engage their services at a moment's notice. Do try to think ahead and not wait until the last possible moment before attempting to book her. Saturday is the most popular night of the week for outings and practically the whole country will be celebrating the beginning of a New Year along with you. Book your babysitter in advance.

2

Getting the Right Person

The easiest way to find a babysitter is to ask among your friends or neighbours. However, this is sometimes not the best solution. Quite apart from the fact that they may be busy or simply unwilling, they may not always be exactly the right person for the job. There are other ways worth trying. Once you have made a truthful assessment of your needs, the type of person you require will dictate, to large extent, where you look for her.

Local groups

Almost any society or group, with a relatively large number of members, is a good source of babysitters. The numbers mean that it is quite likely that someone will be free and willing to help. Groups associated with the church or synagogue, especially young wives' or mothers' clubs, are often rich with potential babysitters. Societies that meet weekly or monthly during the day are well worth tackling if you need a daytime sitter because, obviously, the members are likely to be available then. Do not overlook clubs for old age pensioners, as, very often, elderly people who live far away from their own grandchildren would love to become 'adopted' grandparents. The group you approach should be one whose members most closely approximate to the kind of babysitter you require for your children.

If you are not a member of the group yourself, then it is good manners to approach the leader or chairman for permission to advertise for a babysitter among the members. It is most unlikely that this will be refused. The vicar or chairman might well be able to advise you about a group or society that is new to you.

Neighbours and other parents

Neighbours and other parents are usually marvellous babysitters. They probably know your children well and are familiar with the general life of the family. Other parents are unlikely to be daunted by the prospect of taking charge of your brood and obviously this will contribute vastly to your peace of mind.

Payment is really the only area of difficulty. Friends are often unwilling to accept money for their services. One very good way to avoid any embarrassment is to set up a reciprocal arrangement. This works very well between two people and excellently with a group of, say, six. What it amounts to is that, instead of paying money to your babysitter, you reward her by performing a service for her. This may simply be that you babysit for her and she babysits for you.

Some groups have successfully developed a complex system that includes all sorts of services besides babysitting. One group, for example, has four members, with their husbands acting as associate members. Each member was issued with ten tokens and they drew up a list of jobs on a sliding scale of payment in tokens. These include such things as shopping, meeting the children from school, mowing the lawn (especially suitable for husbands), babysitting and so on. In practice, each service is paid for by another service. Anyone who uses another's services without providing a reciprocal service soon runs out of tokens.

Another similar system suits the needs of a group of mothers with children about the same age. They take it in turns, perhaps in pairs, to look after all the children on a regular weekly basis. Thus, each mother in a group of six can guarantee two free Friday mornings out of three, for example.

Young people

The teenage sons and daughters of friends and neighbours are often willing babysitters. It is a good idea to check with their parents before engaging their services, particularly if it is going to involve a late night.

Scout troops and girl guide groups are good sources. Scouts and guides are encouraged to be responsible and helpful and often relish the opportunity to put their training into practice.

Head teachers are not keen on their pupils taking on jobs in termtime, especially if the job means getting less sleep than usual. Students, on the other hand, are always short of money and have much greater freedom of movement. The students' union of a local college or university will almost certainly be happy to give permission for an advertisement to be pinned on the notice board.

Family

Members of the family are ideal babysitters. Children are usually happy to see aunts, uncles and cousins and doing favours is part of family currency. One word of warning — do not take relatives for granted as babysitters.

The library

Libraries are more than suppliers of free books and librarians are usually highly trained people, anxious to do more than take tickets and stamp the date. Many junior libraries run schemes admirably suited to the needs of a busy mother. These include story time sessions when a group of children can be left in the care of a responsible adult. As well as giving you the benefit of one or two free hours, these sessions are immensely popular with the children and are often packed with interest and information. Subjects vary from fairy stories for the youngest to life in China, for example, for older children. There is also the bonus of introducing your child to the pleasure of reading and the value of the library services.

Advertisements

The essence of a good advertisement, whether it is simply a card in a newsagent's window or an advertisement in a national newspaper, is the same. It should be very clear, state exactly what you require and give your name and where you can be contacted. The main points to cover are, first, that you are looking for a babysitter, when you need someone and for how long, the number of children and their ages, the locality, if this is relevant, and how to contact you. A card in a newsagent's window, for example, might read:

BABYSITTER WANTED
Monday mornings from 10 am to midday, for
John, aged 5, and Susan, aged 3.

Mrs. D. Jones
Tel: Knowlton 741

You can also advertise for an occasional sitter, when it is not possible to be so precise. In a student newspaper you might insert an advertisement like this: **Babysitter** required for occasional evenings. One child, 18 months. Newtown area. Telephone Mary Dawson 0901 24.

Advertisements such as these are quite sufficient for obtaining 'amateur' sitters and can be placed in a number of local places, such as shop windows and launderettes, which usually charge a very small fee, and on notice boards in students' unions, libraries, meeting halls and in the waiting rooms of doctors, dentists and clinics. Do ask permission before pinning them up. Make sure they are legible — type or print clearly in ink or ball point pen. Local newspapers, student magazines, church newsletters and similar publications usually accept two- or three-line advertisements for a fairly small charge.

Advertisements for 'professionals' need a rather different approach and you should study those columns in the national newspapers and specialist magazines before placing an advertisement. The same rules of clarity and exactness apply.

A note on 'professionals'

There are a number of different kinds of people who look after children as a full-time or part-time job. A full investigation of these is really outside the scope of this book. They include childminders, crèches, playschools, nurseries, nannies and au pairs. They fall roughly into two categories — people to whom you take your child and people who come to your home to care for him.

If you decide to employ a nanny, mother's help or au pair, it is very important that you spend time interviewing candidates because you must be sure that you have chosen the right person. Keeping a fairly close eye on progress for the first couple of weeks is common sense and the occasional informal spot check that all is well can reassure you.

Au pairs are usually young, foreign girls, whose main interest is learning about the country and its language. They are not servants on call 24 hours a day and usually they expect to live as members of the family. In return they are prepared to help in the house and with the children, but they must be given free time to attend language classes and pursue their studies and interests.

Nurseries and playschools can be a stimulating experience for a child and can usefully help to bridge the gap between being at home and going to school. They provide supervision, with minimum interference, of lots of different activities such as painting, playing 'shops' or 'houses', sand pits, water games and so on. The children have the opportunity to meet other children and learn to get on with each other. There are often quiet periods for storytelling and more peaceful games. Before choosing a playgroup or nursery, make an appointment to visit one of its sessions. Also check the facilities provided. Good groups provide plenty of activities for children and are usually happy, noisy places. The group leaders recognize the fact that you are anxious to provide the right care for your child and will answer your questions honestly. Rows of solemn faced, well-behaved silent children are a very bad sign. Sometimes a trained nursery nurse may be in charge, and usually the staff are mothers themselves. There are legal regulations governing such places and you should satisfy yourself that these requirements are met. Of course, a fee is charged and this can vary considerably from group to group.

Most playgroups and nurseries are open only in the mornings. Some provide lunch for children but this is not always the case. They do expect the children to be collected promptly at the end of the session.

Crèche facilities usually provide for the care of babies and very young children. Again there are legal regulations governing the way they are run and you should satisfy yourself that these are fulfilled.

Recommendations and references

You should always ask for references from strangers. If you are employing a 'professional', then it is quite reasonable to expect her to provide proof of her qualifications and written references. Remember, however, thay you have no guarantee that these are genuine. If you are using an agency, qualifications and references are their responsibility.

You can be less formal with 'amateurs', but you should be no less scrupulous. Ask for the name and telephone number or address of a previous client. No reputable babysitter will consider this unreasonable. Getting in touch with another mother who has used the babysitter's services can be very helpful and might prevent a potential disaster. Explain why you are telephoning her and ask her about the length of time and frequency with which she employed the babysitter, the number of children, their ages and her general opinion. A telephone call is better than a letter because you will be able to detect any doubts from the tone of voice. Moreover, people tend to be more open in conversation, especially if they have any criticisms, than they are in writing.

The first time you leave a new babysitter in charge should be for a fairly short period and it is sensible not to travel too far away.

Spot checks are an invaluable aid. One, not too obvious, way of checking that all is well is to return earlier than you are expected. Alternatively, you could ask a trusted friend or member of your family to drop by and cast a wary eye on how things are progressing. If you were absent during the day, casually ask your children what they did and how they got on. Children are very perceptive and have no inhibitions in their comments. Finally, do not underestimate the value of your own intuition.

If you do find that you have made a mistake, do not rant and rave, even if the babysitter has done something appalling. Simply tell her that you will not require her services again and do not be tempted to telephone her as a last resort on another occasion, in the vain hope that her bad habits have improved. Also, if you are asked to provide a reference, do not prevaricate and make excuses for a bad babysitter.

3

Ground Rules for Parents

The relationship between you, your babysitter and your children is three-way. After all, once you have gone to all the bother of finding just the right person, sorted out exactly what you want her to do and settled the children, you want to be able to call on her services again. Treat her fairly and she will respond in the same way.

Introducing the children

Most children go through a stage when they cling, more or less literally, to their mothers and are very shy of strangers. Some children continue to be nervous of adults they do not know and all children are likely to be distressed if they wake up in the middle of the night to find that the only adult in the house is someone they have never seen before. In addition, children can be prey to all kinds of secret worries, including a fear that, when their parents go out, they will never return (see Chapter 9, Some Common Problems). Any of these things can turn your outing into a nightmare for the child.

You should always introduce a new babysitter and the children to each other before you go out. If you are planning to put the children to bed yourself, ask the babysitter to come early so that she and the children can meet each other. If this is not possible, suggest that she spends five or ten minutes with you and the children one or two days before. If the children already know their babysitter, there is no need to reintroduce her in this way unless they have not seen her for a long time. You should, however, explain to the children that you are going out and tell them who is coming to look after them. Quite often, they will regard this as something of a treat and you would be wise to adopt a similar attitude. For example, let the children stay up for an extra thirty minutes after getting ready for bed so that they may greet her.

If you know that your child is particularly shy with other adults, do warn your babysitter (but not in front of the child concerned). You should also tell her about any other aspects of his personality that may require some special consideration. Mention such things as distress at the death of a pet, disturbance due to a move to a new house, jealousy of a new baby or difficulties at school. Do not go into great detail but warning of a problem area can smooth the way for both babysitter and child.

If you lead a busy social life, it is a wise precaution to acclimatize your children to your absences as early as possible. If a child is used to meeting different adults and is familiar with being left in the care of a babysitter for short periods, he is unlikely to be upset by longer absences.

Playing fair

Do make it clear to your babysitter before she arrives exactly what the job entails. She may be perfectly willing to take the dog for a walk in addition to amusing the children, but do not spring it upon her as a surprise. Equally, do not just assume she will know what you want her to do without telling her.

If you are paying your sitter, agree the fee in advance. An hourly rate is probably the fairest method. Also, be sure that you have enough cash to pay her when you get home. Do not expect her to have change of a large note or, worse still, to wait until you have been to the bank on the following day.

Heating

Babysitters tend to do just that — sit, for prolonged periods, especially during the evening. Make sure the room, designated sitter's HQ, is warm. Show her where gas and electric fires turn on and off. If you have open fires, make sure that there is an adequate supply of coal and that it is accessible. Show her how the fire 'works' and where to find the poker and other equipment. If you have central heating, give a thought to the timer before you go out. If you normally go to bed at 11 o'clock and the heating switches off at half past, you may return at 2 am and find your babysitter wrapped in coats and scarves, blue around the lips and shivering with cold.

Your home

It is surprising how easy it is to forget that other people are not familiar with the very simple and basic workings of your house or flat. For example, if you expect your babysitter to prepare the children's tea, she probably needs to know how to switch on the cooker, where the can opener is kept and where the saucepans and plates are to be found. She may need to switch on an immersion heater for the children's baths. How will she find the antiseptic and the sticking plaster for a grazed knee? Even the whereabouts of the light switch for the staircase may not be obvious. Think about what your sitter needs to know and make a point of allowing time to tell her.

Food and drink

Your babysitter will certainly want a cup of tea or coffee. Depending on the time of day and how long she will be babysitting, she may well need something to eat.

It is simplest to prepare a tea tray before you go out. Tell her where to find cups and saucers, tea, coffee, sugar and so on. Also tell her where to empty tea leaves and coffee grounds.

The easiest arrangement with food is for your sitter to share any meal she is preparing for the children. Otherwise, sandwiches are generally acceptable and not a lot of trouble for you to prepare. A small plate of biscuits on the tea tray is a friendly touch.

The children

It is important that you provide your sitter with adequate information about her charges. Many a babysitter has had an unfortunate experience when confronted with a child's pet word for going to the lavatory. She is not going to be able to guess what 'need grunties' means, or at least, not in time. And if you leave the children to tell her their bedtimes, you can be sure they will add at least one hour.

Children can be very easily upset by the unexpected and at certain ages are very anxious about their parents' absence (see Chapter 9, Some Common Problems). It is, therefore, especially helpful if your babysitter can, as far as possible, maintain the normal routine. To do this, she needs full information, right down to which cuddly toy normally accompanies your child to bed and whether to leave a lamp on or the curtains partly open.

In Part Two, basic information sheets are included for each age-group and time of day. If you use these to provide precise information about each of your children, then you can be sure that your babysitter has everything she needs to know at her fingertips and can be left fully in control.

Punctuality

It should not need saying that you must be punctual about your return home. Your thirty-minute delay may prevent your babysitter from catching the last train home, and if you said that you would be home at midnight but do not return until nearly 1 am, you may have worried your babysitter unnecessarily and also caused anxiety to her family, who had been expecting her home for the past hour. If, for any reason, you are delayed, let your babysitter know and she will probably be willing to remain for a further hour.

Where you are

The chances are that your babysitter will not need to bother you while you are out. However, emergencies can occur, both in your family and in hers. Moreover, the very nature of an emergency is that it is unexpected. Provide your babysitter with full information about where you will be. For example, if you are going to the theatre, give her the name of the theatre, the telephone number and the numbers of your seats. This may seem unnecessarily fussy, but, if your babysitter does need to contact you, speed is of the essence.

Travelling arrangements

Very often your babysitter will finish her duties late at night. It is customary to make sure that she can get home safely. If she lives within walking distance, it would be courteous if the man of the family saw her home and, equally, he should accompany her to the bus stop or station. Otherwise, drive her home or provide a mini-cab and regard the cost as an investment in goodwill.

Staying overnight

You do not need to make elaborate arrangements if your babysitter is to stay overnight and, indeed, these would only embarrass her. However, do make sure that she is comfortable and make up and air the bed before she arrives. Leave an extra blanket in the room and provide a hot water bottle, unless you have a spare electric blanket. Make sure that there are hangers for her clothes and a clean towel. Check that the light bulbs are working in the spare room, especially if you do not use it very often. If it also serves as a junk room, make sure she can move without banging her shins on hidden obstacles. Provide a portable fire or turn on the radiator before you go out.

Expenses

If your babysitter is going to take the children out, rather than simply stay in the house with them, give her sufficient money to cover the cost of the outing. This may include bus or train fares, entrance fees, the cost of a meal or possibly just an ice-cream. Do remember to take her fares and so on into consideration as well.

Presenting the information

Knowing what information you need to give your babysitter is one thing, but making sure you have included it all is a different matter. Also, if you reel off a great list of 'wheres' and 'hows' halfway out of the front door, there is little chance of her remembering even half of what you have said. The most reliable and efficient way of ensuring that everything is covered is to make a list.

Check-lists and information sheets are included throughout the book. Together they supply sufficient information to enable your babysitter to find what she needs about the house, to look after the children without any problems and to cope speedily and efficiently if an emergency should occur. Your main responsibility is to make sure that you have supplied the information she will need.

The following check-list, About the House, can be adapted to suit your particular needs. For example, there is no need to give information about saucepans and cooking utensils if your babysitter is not required to prepare a meal.

About the House

General

Telephone
Spare light bulbs
Matches
Candles/torch
Sheets (in case of accidents)
Towels
First aid box/cupboard
Door keys
Hot water bottle(s)
Safety gate
Toy box/cupboard
Playpen
Immersion heater
No-go areas (e.g. sitting room, parents' bedroom)

Kitchen

Tea/coffee
Sugar
Salt
Children's food
Children's drinks

Kettle

Saucepans etc.

Wire strainer

Plates etc.

Knives, forks etc.

Tablecloth

Plastic mats etc.

Rubbish bin

Floorcloth

Pets

Food

Drink

Walk

Lead

Basket/box

Other notes (e.g. no-go areas)

Show where they are and how they work:

Fires

Television

Radio

Light switches

Locks and bolts

Cooker

Electric blender/food mill

Coffee maker

Washing-up machine

Electric blanket(s)

4

Ground Rules for Babysitters

It is obvious, although quite often overlooked, that before the parents employing you as a babysitter leave you in charge, you should establish exactly what you are in charge of. Some of your responsibilities will not change whatever the situation or the age of the children. First and foremost, you are in charge of their welfare and safety. This is your prime responsibility and everything else takes second place to it. If you are babysitting at someone else's house, which is usually the case, you are also in charge of that.

Caring for the children may simply involve the presence of a responsible adult (you) while the parents are out. However, in the evening you might be asked to prepare the children's tea for example, or bath them before putting them to bed. If you are babysitting during the day, you might be expected to take them to the park or to play with them in the house.

Sometimes, parents require other duties from babysitters, in addition to the obvious ones listed above. The tasks vary from family to family and from babysitter to babysitter. It is important to establish exactly what is expected of you before you are left alone to get on with it.

However, if a child in your care seems to be ill or shows symptoms of abdominal pain for no particular reason, then you should telephone the parents at once.

Guideline information sheets for parents to complete are provided throughout this book. They are designed to include all the information you might require during the course of babysitting — from details of where things can be found in the house, through the routines of the children in your care to emergency telephone numbers and accident procedures. Do make sure that the parents have provided this information, that it is up-to-date and that they have remembered to give it to you.

Someone else's home

Leaving their children and their home, probably the most precious things in their lives, implies considerable trust in you on the part of the parents. Of course you are intending to act responsibly about the children, but you should also give some thought to your behaviour in someone else's home.

The simplest rule to follow is do not do anything that you would resent someone else doing in your home. This applies equally to such obvious things as looking through the correspondence on someone else's desk or poking in cupboards that do not concern you, as it does to less obvious but more likely activities, such as putting wet glasses down on a polished table or scattering biscuit crumbs over the sofa. In other words, always take special care in someone else's home, particularly with food, drink and lighted cigarettes. If you do break something or cause some sort of damage accidentally, tell the parents when they return.

A common way for babysitters to pass the time is to watch the television or listen to the radio. If the parents forget to show you how these work, do ask them. Record players and sound systems can be easily damaged and are best left alone.

You should not need to use the telephone, except if the children become ill or in cases of emergency, when you might have to contact the parents or call a doctor, or if you need to inform your family that you have been delayed. You should never use it to make personal calls, even if you are willing to pay for them. Equally, you should not ask friends to telephone you at the house where you are babysitting.

You should, of course, answer the telephone if it rings while you are in charge. State the number clearly, explain that the parents are out and that you are the babysitter. Offer to take a message, making sure that you have a pad and pencil near the telephone (see Babysitter's Basic Equipment). Take the caller's name and, if it is not clear, ask him to spell it. Write the message down immediately and, if the caller wants to be called back when the parents return, take his telephone number. Read the message back, especially any numbers, before you hang up. Remember to give the message to the parents when they return.

Exercise caution if someone calls at the house when you are in charge. If there is a chain on the door, use it, especially in the evenings. You should explain that the parents are out and that you are the babysitter but, unless you know the caller or you have been warned to expect him or her, do not let strangers into the house, however plausible the excuse. Wait for the caller to identify himself. Be polite but firm. A genuine friend or neighbour is unlikely to be offended by such treatment and the absent parents will appreciate your vigilance. By all means, offer to take the name of the caller so that you can inform the parents when they return. Write it down on your notepad.

Remember that anyone can claim to be a meter reader or a policeman and even a uniform is no guarantee of genuineness. Ask to see some form of official identification and do not let the caller in unless you are fully satisfied. It is better to refuse entry to a genuine detective than to let in a false one, and he will be the first to admit it.

If repairmen or deliveries are expected, you should have been informed in advance. Once again, let them identify themselves rather than simply assuming they are the people you expect. If you are asked to sign for something, make sure that you indicate that the contents have not been inspected. If necessary, write this above your signature.

In most cases, the above precautions will prove to have been unnecessary and the callers will have been quite genuine. Nevertheless, thieves and other criminals have used all kinds of pretexts to gain entry. Once they are in the house there is not much you can do. Also, keep an eye open if you do decide to let callers in, especially if there is more than one. When you are showing one man where the meter is, the other could be emptying your purse or stuffing the silver in his tool bag.

Do not worry about being suspicious or appearing unfriendly. Do not let embarrassment prevent you from insisting on identification. Be polite but do not give in to bluster. The golden rule is — if in doubt, keep them out.

Punctuality

It is absolutely essential that you arrive at the time agreed. Apart from causing inconvenience to the parents, who may have booked theatre or train tickets, your lateness immediately creates an impression of unreliability. If some unforeseen circumstance, such as a flat tyre, delays you, telephone the parents to explain the situation. They may then have time either to help you with your problem or, if necessary, to try and make alternative arrangements.

The parents' viewpoint

You may have very strong views on bringing up children, especially if you do not have any of your own. However, babysitting is not the time for practical experiment. You are employed to take care of the children in the parents' absence and you should, as far as possible, respect the parents' viewpoint and abide by the 'house rules'. For example, parents might censor a child's television viewing and ban programmes with scenes of violence, while you might feel that he needs to discriminate for himself and should learn about all aspects of life, including the unpleasant ones.

Your viewpoint may well be perfectly valid and reasonable, but this is not the time to pursue it. First of all, the parents have the right to decide how their children are to be brought up. Secondly, by introducing a wholly new approach you can confuse the child and possibly distress him. Thirdly, you are unlikely to know all the factors involved. The banned television programme that you think is fairly harmless might trouble a sensitive child give him nightmares for several weeks afterwards.

Keeping to the plan

It is very important that you stick to whatever plans you and the parents have made if you are taking the children out. Whether you are planning a day trip to the zoo or simply an hour in the park, you must follow the prearranged timetable. A lot of unnecessary distress can be caused by arriving home an hour later than arranged, simply because you decided to stop for tea. If you do need to change the plan, telephone the parents to let them know what the changes are. If they are not available, make sure that your change of plan at least gets you home at the same time as before. If this is not possible, then make sure you telephone the parents at the time they are expecting you home.

Boyfriends and girlfriends

Teenagers particularly, often like to babysit in pairs and this can be perfectly satisfactory. However, you should check with the parents and, if they refuse permission for your girlfriend or boyfriend to accompany you, abide by their decision. You are in a position of trust and it is an abuse of that trust to invite your boyfriend round half an hour after they have gone out.

If you are sharing your babysitting responsibilities with another boy or girl, keep in mind the reason why you are there. It is easy to get carried away playing games, watching television or listening to music. Babysitting can be very enjoyable but enjoying yourself is not your main purpose.

Finally, it should not need saying that babysitting must not be regarded as an opportunity to behave in a manner of which your own parents would disapprove.

Babysitter's Basic Equipment

Notepad

Pen/pencil

Torch
(in case of power cuts)

Newspaper or list of television/radio programmes and times
(for children and self)

Apron/overall
(for protection when feeding, bathing etc.)

Book/magazine
(to pass the time)

Reserve cash for mini-cab
(in case of emergencies)

Change for coin telephone
(in case of emergencies)

PART TWO

5

Young Babies

Very young babies do not really differentiate between night and day, at least not in their behaviour. Their time is divided between prolonged periods of sleep and wakefulness, when they need to be fed. As they grow older, they stay awake longer and they spend some time playing with simple toys, their feet and their clothes and watching what is going on around them.

Babysitting requirements are very similar whatever the time of day, although, as babies grow older, the demands will become greater during the day than at night. Parents should complete an information sheet on the baby and his routine, based on the suggestions given at the end of this chapter.

Feeding (Parents' notes)

If you are breastfeeding, there is no need to be housebound. It may be possible to time your outings so that you leave after one feed and return before the next is due. If this is your plan, it is a good idea to leave a drink of boiled water or fruit juice ready, in case your baby wakes up hungry before you get back. There is no reason why you should not occasionally go out for longer periods than the interval between feeds. (It is not possible to do this regularly, as the lack of stimulation will discourage the milk supply.) In this case, you will need to leave a bottle feed ready for the babysitter to give. This can either be made from a commercial brand of dried milk or be expressed breast milk.

If possible, you should prepare the feed yourself and store it in the refrigerator. You will then be sure that everything has been cleaned properly and sterilized and the mixture made up in the correct proportions.

Provide clear instructions about the time your baby usually feeds, the temperature of the milk and his feeding habits, such as whether he is a slow feeder. Also, if your baby is usually breastfed, tell the babysitter so that she is prepared to persevere with the unfamiliar bottle.

Feeding (Babysitter's notes)

Many mothers like to prepare the baby's bottle before they go out and leave it ready in the refrigerator. All you have to do, in this case, is warm the milk to the desired temperature and give it to the baby. It is sensible to suggest this to the mother in advance, especially if you are not used to preparing bottles yourself.

The information sheet will tell you the usual temperature for the baby's milk. Older babysitters, especially those who brought up children some years ago when milk was always warmed to blood heat, may be surprised to find that some babies prefer cold milk.

If there is an electric bottle warmer, make sure that you are shown how it works before the parents go out and follow their instructions. Otherwise, heat the bottle in a saucepan of hot, but not boiling, water for a few minutes. Test the milk by sprinkling a few drops on the back of your hand, but do not touch the teat itself. If the milk is at blood heat, it will feel neither hot nor cold. If it feels hot, cool it slightly under running cold water and test the milk again on the back of your hand. It is better to give a slightly cool feed than one that is too hot and hurts the baby.

Try to allow a minimum of thirty minutes without interruptions to feed the baby. Protect your clothes and the baby's before you start. Sit in a comfortable chair with a sloping back and arms, which will help to support your arms. It is probably a good idea to use the same chair as the mother uses. Hold the baby in one arm with his head raised. This is important because, otherwise, he might choke. Make sure that you are comfortable and relaxed. If you are tense, the baby will respond and feeding time will turn into a futile battle. Avoid sitting directly under a bright light. Remember to remove the disc from within the teat before you start because this will block the milk flow.

Offer him the bottle, keeping it slightly tilted so that the teat is always full of milk. This stops him sucking in a lot of air and later suffering extreme discomfort from wind. Every now and then, gently disengage the teat to allow some air to flow back into the bottle. The baby's sucking creates a vacuum in the bottle which will prevent him obtaining any more milk.

Babies feed at different speeds, but almost all of them are easily distracted, even when very hungry. Most like to pause occasionally to gaze around or to play a little. This is, after all, an opportunity for cuddling and contact. If he goes on playing for too long, however, he may need reminding of his bottle. The best way to do this is gently to stroke the cheek nearest to you. He will automatically turn towards you and you can offer the bottle again. Do not be tempted to thrust the teat into his mouth. If he refuses the proferred teat, this probably means that he has had enough.

Never leave a baby alone with a bottle, even for a few seconds. In that brief time, he could choke. If you are interrupted, remove the bottle and transfer the baby to a safe place, such as his cot.

When he has finished feeding, discard any milk remaining. You should never keep it, even for half an hour, because warm milk is a wonderful breeding ground for bacteria. Rinse the bottle and teat in cold water.

Most babies like a little cuddle after they have been fed and, if they are going to bring up some wind, this is the time they will do it. Cuddle the baby in whatever is the most comfortable position for both of you, but do not be obsessive about making him 'burp'.

Some babies regurgitate a little milk after, or even during, feeding. This is quite different from vomiting and is perfectly normal. It is slightly messy but this should not be a problem if you have protected your clothes and the baby's before starting to give the bottle.

Although it is advisable for mothers to prepare the feed in advance, there may be occasions when this is not practical or there is simply not time. There are two basic rules. The first is to ensure that everything is sterile and the second is to follow precisely the manufacturer's instructions.

First wash your hands thoroughly. Wash the bottle in hot water and detergent, using a bottle brush to get in all the corners. Rinse thoroughly in running water. Sprinkle the inside and outside of the teat with salt and rub it with your fingers until no stickiness remains. Rinse it thoroughly in running water and squirt some water through the hole to ensure that it is not blocked.

The bottle and teat can either be sterilized in boiling water or in sterilizing solution. They must be boiled for ten minutes or soaked for three hours. Follow the manufacturer's instructions for making up the sterilizing solution. Many mothers use a special sterilizing unit which holds several bottles at a time. Make sure that you know how it works. However, it is more likely that, even if the mother has not been able to prepare the feed, she will have washed and sterilized the equipment. Never use a bottle straight from a cupboard or the sink. If the time is short, use the boiling water method.

Follow the manufacturer's instructions for making up the feed. Level the scoop with a knife blade and never add more milk powder than is recommended.

Solid foods (Parents' notes)

Regardless of any convictions you may have about always cooking fresh food, this is an occasion when canned, prepared baby food is invaluable. If you insist on using fresh ingredients, then either you should prepare the meal in advance or, if your babysitter will be preparing a meal anyway, make sure it is one that all the children, whatever their ages, can eat.

Solid foods (Babysitter's notes)

The amount of preparatory work depends on what food is being given to the baby. Proprietary baby foods are already sieved and require no preparation, although some mothers like to warm them slightly. Cereals only need mashing up with a little warm milk and boiled eggs are very straightforward. Make sure that you do not serve eggs too hot and burn the baby's mouth. Allow them to cool to lukewarm.

Once he is happily accepting solids, a baby can eat more or less anything that the family eats. If he is going to share a meal that you are preparing for older children, you will need to mash his portion to a fairly fine pulp. The younger the baby, the less able he is to cope with lumps. A food mill or electric blender is the simplest way of doing this, but rubbing the mixture through a wire strainer also works adequately.

Babies generally do not like spices and flavourings and you should not add salt to their food because their kidneys cannot deal with it. Baby foods, therefore, taste unappetisingly bland to the adult palate. Do not let this worry you.

Protect both your clothes and the baby's and fasten him securely into his high chair. Feed him with a teaspoon, allowing him to finish one mouthful before popping in the next. When he has had enough, he will almost certainly push the spoon away and, if you force any more into his mouth, he will spit it out.

The information sheet will include instructions on the baby's drink, usually milk or fruit juice. Use a special feeder cup with a lid and spout, if he has one, or at the very least, a plastic beaker, as he is quite likely to hurl it across the room without any warning.

If he finishes his meal with a piece of cheese, toast, peeled apple or other hard food that he can gnaw, do not let him walk about with it or leave him alone, in case he chokes.

Changing (Parents' notes)

Make sure that your babysitter knows where all the equipment is and include it on your information sheet. If she is inexperienced, it might be a good idea to leave a nappy already folded or to buy a packet of disposable nappies, if you do not normally use them, for just such occasions.

Changing (Babysitter's notes)

Some babies scream almost instantly their nappies are wet or soiled, while others seem quite oblivious to the dampness around their bottoms. However, it is not a good idea to leave a baby lying in a wet or soiled nappy, as this can lead to nappy rash. Many babies soil their nappies after feeding and this is a good time to check to see if a change is necessary.

Before you start, collect all the equipment you are going to need in one place. You can change the baby on your lap, but putting him on a flat surface is usually easier. Protect the surface or your lap with a towel or changing pad. Lie the baby on his back and give him a toy to play with and to distract his attention. This is a particularly useful ploy with those babies who hate having their nappies changed and seem deliberately to obstruct the process.

Remove the dirty nappy and put this on one side to deal with afterwards. Remove and close any safety pins and put them out of the baby's reach. Clean the baby's bottom, using a tissue or cotton wool and warm water or baby lotion. You should always wipe a baby girl's bottom away from the vagina to avoid the risk of infection. Dry the baby's bottom, including the folds of flesh around the thighs. Use gentle, dabbing movements when washing and drying, rather than rubbing which might make the skin sore. Rub in a little zinc and castor oil cream, or whatever else is usually used. Talcum powder is not necessary and can cake in the folds of the skin. If you are using powder, do not shake the container violently, as it is dangerous for the baby to inhale it.

Disposable nappies are simplest. They wrap around the baby and fasten with self-sealing tapes. You do not need to lift the baby up completely, just raise his bottom and slide the nappies in and out.

If you are using a towelling nappy, fold it in the following way. Fold one side into the middle and fold the other side over it to give three layers. Then fold the bottom third up, so that the bottom part of the nappy has six layers of cloth and the top part has three layers. Wrap the nappy around the baby with the thicker portion at the front for boys and for girls who sleep on their fronts. Put the thicker part at the back for girls who sleep on their backs. Pin the nappy at each side, holding the cloth away from the baby's skin to avoid pricking him. Make sure the pins are securely fastened and slip plastic pants over the top. (See the diagram on page 38.)

Sometimes, very small babies have gauze or muslin nappies. Fold these in the same way as the towelling nappy above. When it is in position, pin a towelling nappy around the baby, like a skirt.

If you are using a nappy liner, simply position this in the folded nappy before wrapping it around the baby.

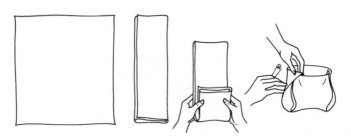

Folding a nappy

Discard soiled or wet disposable nappies. Damp cloth nappies and soiled cloth nappies are usually soaked in separate buckets of sterilizing solution. Flush the contents of a soiled nappy down the toilet before putting it into the bucket of solution to soak.

Bathing (Parents' notes)

It is not essential to bath a very young baby every day, provided his head and bottom are washed daily. It would, therefore, be better to cancel his bath on the day you are going out, especially if your babysitter is not very experienced with small babies. Young babies dislike being bathed and the event might prove to be thoroughly wretched and frightening for both parties. Alternatively, you could bath the baby before the sitter arrives.

Bedtime (Parents' notes)

Provide your sitter with information about your baby's sleeping habits, his cot, his clothes and, very important, whether he sleeps on his front or his back. Babies do not readily change their habits and, if he is put to bed on his back but usually sleeps on his front, he may cry for hours to the real bewilderment of his babysitter.

Bedtime (Babysitter's notes)

Putting a baby to bed is a relatively straightforward process. Make sure the bedroom is warm and change his nappy before you settle him down. The information sheet will tell you whether he normally sleeps on his front or his back, so put him in his cot whichever way he prefers. Pillows are not necessary, but he does need warm bedclothes tucked around him. Young babies especially, like to be securely tucked in. Occasionally, a baby throws off his bedclothes and you should check during the course of the evening that he has not become uncovered.

Some babies cry for a few minutes after being put down, but they soon drop off to sleep. There is no need to creep around the house on tiptoe. Babies sleep for many hours both during the day and at night and have to become accustomed to ordinary household noises. Use your common sense about the television. Do not have the volume turned up too high if you are watching a programme with guns banging and police sirens wailing but, equally, you do not need to turn it down so low that you can barely hear it.

If a baby wakes up, he can do one of three things. He can go back to sleep, lie quietly looking around him or cry. If he does either of the first two, you need not concern yourself. Babies require different amounts of sleep, just as adults do, so, if he wants to investigate his toes or watch a mobile over his crib, do not feel that you must get him back to sleep at all costs. On the other hand, when he cries, he is communicating some sort of need to you.

This may be an obvious practical need you can deal with easily. If he wakes up near his feeding time, then he is probably hungry and this may also be the reason for crying if he took less milk than usual during the previous feed. Remember too, that babies can get thirsty, especially in hot weather. Another common reason for crying is a dirty nappy. It is worth checking a crying baby to see if his nappy needs changing. However, never wake up a baby to change him. If he is sleeping peacefully in a soiled nappy, then it is clearly not worrying him.

A baby may cry simply because he is not sleepy and is bored lying in a darkened room, especially if he sleeps on his front and all he can see is the side of his crib, or he may be lonely and want a cuddle. In both these cases, pick him up, cuddle him and, perhaps, play a game or even sing to him for a few minutes.

Another reason for crying is that he is uncomfortable. The bedclothes may have slipped off, if he is a restless sleeper, and he may be cold. The bottom sheet may be rucked up and causing him discomfort.

These are the most common reasons for crying and usually the cause becomes obvious quite quickly. When you have dealt with the problem, whether by changing his nappy or singing a lullaby, put him back in his crib and he will probably go to sleep. Further information on persistent crying is given in Chapter 9, Some Common Problems.

Playing (Parents' notes)

On your information sheet include details of the whereabouts of your baby's play mat, bouncer chair and so on. It is probably worth pointing out that even small babies like to play, as inexperienced babysitters may not realize that they do anything other than eat and sleep.

Playing (Babysitter's notes)

Play is a serious business for babies because this is how they find out about the world around them and, in fact, that there is a world around them. A bored baby is a difficult baby, so when he is awake he needs to occupy his developing mind and begin to learn about all the skills he will eventually acquire.

The room must be warm and free of draughts and you should never leave him alone propped up in a chair. If he has a bouncer chair, make sure the straps are securely fastened but not too tight. You can leave him alone in this for short periods, but when he is approaching the crawling stage, he will be able to bounce himself right over. Play should be supervised, except when he is lying in his cot. He will also be happy watching you and listening to you, if you talk to him.

Some of the best games for babies are those played sitting on your lap. Traditional favourites, like 'This little piggy went to market', remain ever popular and a baby loves to hear your voice, whether you are talking or singing. It does not matter if you cannot sing a note, he will love it.

Playing is an opportunity to use his arms and legs, so let him have plenty of freedom to wave them around. A soft play mat on the floor of a warm room is ideal for this. Make sure that it is not too close to a fire or radiator and give him a toy to occupy his attention.

Do not let him grab hold of anything sharp or breakable. Babies like to grasp things and go through a stage of putting everything in their mouths. Keep small objects, like beads and peanuts, out of his reach. Also, avoid letting him play with older children's toys. Apart from causing trouble, because children are very possessive about their toys, something suitable for, say, a three-year-old, can be dangerous for a baby.

Taking babies out (Parents' notes)

Do not suggest to an inexperienced babysitter that she takes your baby out in his pram or pushchair. To someone not used to it, manoeuvring a pram through busy streets is very hazardous and should not be encouraged. Far better for your peace of mind that she looks after the baby indoors.

If an outing is unavoidable, make sure you explain where to find suitable clothing and also pram clothes. Show the babysitter where the pram or pushchair is kept and how it works. Remember to tell her how the brakes are applied, and stress the importance of using them.

Taking babies out (Babysitters' notes)

It is unlikely that you will be asked to take the baby out. If this should be necessary, there are various points to watch. Wrap the baby up well, depending on the weather, and settle him snugly and securely in the pram. Once he can sit up, he must always wear a pram harness.

Prams and pushchairs are difficult to control. Pushchairs can tip over quite easily and great care must be taken. You should find out exactly how the brakes work before setting out — and do not fail to apply them properly.

Young Babies *Information Sheet*

Baby's name
_____

Baby's age
_____

Timetable

Sleeping
_____

Feed
_____

Drink
_____

Awake/playing
_____

Feeding

Normally breastfed/bottle fed
_____

Fast/slow feeder
_____

Average amount taken at each feed
_____

Prepared bottle
_____

Temperature of milk (blood heat/cold)
_____

Electric bottle warmer/saucepan (N.B. show how bottle warmer works)
_____

Bib
_____

Usual chair, footstool etc. for feeding

Tendency to regurgitate milk during/after feeding

Preparing the feed:

    Dried milk

    Bottle and teat

    Bottle brush

    Detergent

    Salt

    Sterilizing solution

    Sterilizing unit

    Measuring scoop

Solid food

Food (and temperature)

Drink

High chair (and harness)

Bib

Bowl, feeder cup etc.

Electric blender/food mill

Changing

Changing pad

Nappies and pins

Disposable nappies

Nappy liners

Plastic pants

Bowl (for water)

Baby lotion

Zinc and castor oil/petroleum jelly etc.

Cotton wool/tissues

Bucket (wet nappies)

Bucket (soiled nappies)

Bin (disposable nappies)

Usual sleeping position (girls only)

Bedtime

Bedroom

Heater

Cot

Clothes

Usual sleeping position (front/back)

Playing

Play mat

Bouncer chair etc.

Favourite game

Favourite toy

Outings

Pram/pushchair – brakes

Protective covering/cat net

Clothing, bonnet, mits etc.

Pram clothes

Other

Prepared drink (water/fruit juice)

Special problems (e.g. teething/remedies)

Clean clothes

6

Toddlers and Young Children – Evenings

Once children are past the baby stage, the care required from a babysitter, or parent for that matter, varies considerably depending on the time of day. The tasks for an evening babysitter may include giving the children their tea, entertaining them for a little while, bathing them and putting them to bed. On the other hand, the parents may not go out until the children are in bed.

Parents should provide adequate information about each of their children and basic information sheets are included at the end of this chapter.

Tea (Parents' notes)

It is not always possible to time your outings so that you can give the children their tea before you leave. Often, they will enjoy the novelty of teatime with a different adult in charge. However, you should endeavour to make the process as painless as possible. Either leave a meal ready, requiring nothing more than heating up, or provide clear instructions for a simple meal. Details about where to find saucepans, plates and so on should be included in your About the House information sheet (see Chapter 3, Ground Rules for Parents).

Tea (Babysitter's notes)

Protect the table, yourself and the children's clothes before you start. Supervise thorough hand washing because hands often play a major part in transferring food from plate to mouth. Make sure the children are all seated properly before you put the food on the table. Sit the children in their usual places, not only because the chairs are likely to be the right height, but also because it will prevent any quarrels about who sits next to whom.

Do not heap the food on the plates. If a child is still hungry when he has emptied his plate, then he can have some more. There is no reason why a baby in a highchair should not be fed at the same time as older brothers and sisters, but younger babies, who have not yet tackled solids, are better fed quietly and separately when you can concentrate on one thing at a time.

From about one year old onwards, most children like to feed themselves. This may be something of a messy business, but it is best to let them get on with it. Cut up the food into bite-size pieces and do not worry if an occasional thumb helps push an elusive bit of potato on to the spoon. Do not insist on feeding the child yourself, to avoid the mess or to speed up the process. You will only frustrate him and he may refuse to eat altogether. However, if he is getting bored or having difficulties, a little assistance may be required.

From the age of about two, children begin to understand the concept of table manners. Younger children really cannot grasp what is expected of them and tend to regard food with the same glee as a mud puddle. It takes children time to learn the niceties of good behaviour at the table, so do not expect them to behave perfectly and do not snap at them if they do something wrong. However, you should put a firm stop to squabbles between brothers and sisters before they reach the food slinging stage. Do not expect younger ones to sit on after they have finished, if older brothers or sisters are still eating. They quickly grow bored and the wait seems endless to them.

Playing and television (Parents' notes)

Your information sheet, About the House (see Chapter 3, Ground Rules for Parents), should provide details about the toy box or cupboard and should also include any 'no-go areas', such as the sitting room. If you have strong convictions about television, make sure your babysitter knows them. It is also a good idea to make a note on your information sheet about the times and the programmes your children like to watch, as she may not be familiar with them.

Playing and television (Babysitter's notes)

Children will often play quite happily on their own, as long as you provide a reassuring presence. They do not always want your help, which they regard as unwarranted interference. Young children do not play together right from the start, although they may play separate games alongside each other. Learning to share is a long process which does not come readily and should not be forced.

The information sheet will tell you where children are allowed to play and, under no circumstances, should they play freely in the kitchen. This is the most dangerous room in the house, not only because small fingers can find their way into drawers full of sharp cutlery, but also because a model car underfoot when you are carrying a scalding hot saucepan could be catastrophic.

Most children have more toys than they can possibly play with. However, it is a good idea to have one or two simple games up your sleeve to ease you through difficult moments and to provide diversions and entertainment. Drawing pictures with crayons or painting is always popular with children from about eighteen months old onwards. Protect the table and carpet with thick wads of newspaper and cover the child's clothes with a plastic pinafore or overalls. Cutting up an old magazine or greetings cards for a scrap book is cheap and simple and appeals to children over three. Make sure the scissors have rounded ends and that surfaces are protected from paste. Snap is also a perennial favourite for this age-group. Nursery rhymes and action songs are nearly always successful and your audience will join in with uncritical gusto.

It is sensible to encourage children to put their toys away before they go to bed. Deal with pots of water and messy newspaper yourself. A good way to enlist the children's assistance is to suggest that they make everything nice and tidy for when mummy and daddy return.

There are a number of excellent television programmes designed especially for this age-group, so make sure you know what time they begin. Switch the television on and off yourself and make sure it is properly adjusted. Do not let the children sit too close to the screen and it is a good idea to watch the programmes with them. First of all, you can keep an eye on them and join in the songs and games. Second, if something has upset or frightened one of the children, you know what it was. Third, the programme might suggest something you and the children can do together (or that you might like to use another time). When the programmes you have planned to watch have finished, switch off and embark on some other activity. Do not settle down to watch adult programmes while the children are still around.

Toilets and potties (Parents' notes)

On your information sheets about each child you should include details of whether he uses the toilet or potty, where it is, whether he is still prone to accidents or is fully trained, and if he uses a pet word when he wants to go to the toilet. A child who has only just learned to ask for his potty needs immediate attention and can be very upset if he has an accident, just because his babysitter did not understand what he was asking. You may know what he means when he says 'quick!', but she will not unless you tell her. This is a very good reason for teaching your child to use conventional expressions from an early age. Finally, you should tell your babysitter if you normally 'lift' a child at night to use his potty.

Toilets and potties (Babysitter's notes)

Once a child has learned to use the ordinary toilet, he usually likes to be left to manage on his own. He may not always be totally successful, but he will never learn if he is not allowed to try. It is worth checking that all is well, especially if he has been missing for some time, and do ensure that he has washed his hands afterwards.

A child who is still using a potty requires help. Once he asks, his need is immediate and you should take him straight to it. Sit him on it and stay with him while he uses it. A kind word afterwards, such as 'well done', encourages him, but do not lavish extravagant praise or the whole thing gets totally out of proportion.

When young children are deeply absorbed in their games or in a television programme, they can overlook the need to go to the toilet. Tell-tale signs are crossed legs, jumping up and down and holding the front of the trousers or dress. Quietly ask the child if he wants to go to the toilet or to use his potty, using whatever word is familiar to him.

However, if you think a child does want to use his potty and, although you have put him on it, there are no signs that he is going to perform, do not leave him sitting there for ages. He will only become miserable or fall asleep. Try again later.

Almost all children go through a stage of playing with the contents of their potties. These are extremely interesting and not at all disgusting to young children. If you find one of your charges engaged in such an activity, do not make a huge fuss. Be matter-of-fact in removing the offending article and cleaning up the child.

Any child can have an accident through over-excitement, shyness or worry. Once again, the rule is not to fuss. The child will probably be embarrassed and upset and you can reassure him with your manner much more than with words. Make it clear that 'these things happen' and that no blame is attached to him. Try not to be too brisk whisking sheets off the bed or getting him into clean clothes and a friendly smile is always a big help.

Bathtime (Parents' notes)

Your information sheet should include details of bath times, whether more than one child is bathed at the same time, the whereabouts of bath toys, towels, soap and so on. If your child dislikes having his hair washed, and many children hate it, then it is worth giving this a miss on babysitting nights.

Bathtime (Babysitter's notes)

Most children enjoy their baths, especially if there is time for playing and splashing about. Make sure that you are well protected and do not let the play get out of hand so that the entire bathroom is soaked. However, the bathroom is fairly easy to clean up afterwards and not much damage can be done.

Always run the cold water first. A small child can jump into a bath, thinking that it is ready, and be badly scalded if the hot water is run first. Only partly fill the bath to minimize splash-over. Collect together everything you need, including soap, towels, bath toys, nightclothes and slippers. Get the business of washing completed first and then the children can enjoy playing with boats, fish and plastic cups before they are dried. Do not leave children alone in the bath. They can slide over and injure themselves or even knock themselves out and drown. Also they can be badly scalded if they turn on the hot tap while you are not looking.

Dry the child thoroughly after the bath and do not let him get cold. Put him in his nightclothes and wrap him up well in a warm dressing gown and slippers.

Bedtime (Parents' notes)

Include the 'regulation' bedtime on your information sheet and also provide details of the normal routine, such as nightly prayers or a bedtime story. You should also let your babysitter know if your child normally sleeps with a favourite toy. Other details on the information sheet should include special instructions, such as leaving a door open or a lamp on.

Bedtime (Babysitter's notes)

Some children, especially if they have had a busy day, are quite happy to snuggle under the blankets when bedtime comes. Others seem to regard bedtime as a challenge and, however tired they may be, continually plead for 'just five more minutes'.

Approach bedtime firmly but without anticipating trouble. It is a good idea to give a warning about fifteen minutes before the deadline. Set a kitchen timer for those who have not yet learned to tell the time. It is sensible to introduce a quiet activity for the last half hour, as children are much less likely to settle if they are excited after a boisterous game.

It is not a serious problem if bedtime is delayed by ten minutes or so and may be regarded as a special treat to compensate for the parents' absence. However, it can cause real trouble if you do not follow the usual procedures or try to skip part of the bedtime ritual. Ignore this at your peril.

Fill hot water bottles, if these are needed, half an hour before bedtime to take the chill off the sheets. You should never use boiling water and, if you are going to leave the bottles in the beds when the children get in, make sure they are not so hot that they burn sensitive skin. Switch on any heaters in the bedrooms, if necessary, at the same time.

See that the children go to the toilet and, if they are not having baths, wash their hands and faces. Teeth should be brushed last thing, after any bedtime drinks.

Some children like to say prayers out loud before getting into bed. They are usually very earnest about this, so do try to control any desire to laugh at the sincere request to God to 'make the goldfish good'.

The theory behind the bedtime story is that the child, curled up in the warmth of the bed, will gradually grow sleepier listening to a quiet voice, until he eventually dozes off. However, in practice it does not always work this way. Select the story beforehand and decide how long you plan to sit and read. For children of this age-group, one short story is better than a chapter of a longer one. They never seem to get bored hearing the same favourite story over and over again, even when they have reached the stage of knowing it word for word. Beware of any attempts to shorten or change the story, because you will be detected and accused immediately.

Settle the child in bed and do not start until he is lying still and comfortable, bearing in mind all the time that the aim of the exercise is to get him off to sleep. If possible, turn out the main light and read by the light of a lamp. It is better if you can sit on a chair by the side, rather than actually on the bed. You can give full rein to all your dramatic abilities without any fear of accusations of 'hamming'. Use different voices for each of the characters and do not forget to show the pictures to the child at the appropriate moment. Remember that part of the child's pleasure lies in your apparent sharing of his enjoyment, so do not be dismissive in your reading just because the story is simple and predictable.

Making up your own story is just as good as reading someone else's and not as difficult as it sounds. Keep the plot simple and, whatever trials and tribulations plague the hero or heroine in the course of the story, give it a happy ending. Children like stories about other children and make sure all the characters have names. You can encourage the child to help make up the story by asking questions like, 'And what do you think happened next?' and 'Can you guess what was in the mysterious blue bottle?' This can be great fun but be careful not to let the child become too excited and wakeful or you defeat the object of the storytelling. Also bear in mind that too many lurid and horrific details may cause nightmares later. This is equally true of stories read from a book.

When you have finished the story, close the book or make it clear that you have reached the end. Do not be persuaded to tell or read 'just one more'. Settle the child down and say goodnight. (Most children like a goodnight kiss.) The information sheet will include instructions about opening the window, leaving a lamp burning, leaving the door ajar or whatever. When you have seen to these, leave the room and let the child get to sleep. Resist the temptation to look in ten minutes later to see if he is awake.

If possible, keep household sounds to a minimum and turn down the volume of the television set for about the first thirty minutes after putting the child to bed. Children are more sensitive to household noises than babies, perhaps because they understand what they mean. The sounds of older brothers or sisters playing, or laughter from a television comedy, can tempt a child out of bed, or, at least, make it difficult for him to get to sleep. Avoid a confrontation with a pyjama-clad figure, if possible, by allowing him to get off to sleep undisturbed. Once he is asleep, he is unlikely to be woken by ordinary domestic noises.

Constant checking on the child throughout the evening is not necessary. It is probably worth looking round the door of the bedroom once or twice, to make sure that all is well and that he has not thrown all his bedclothes on the floor (some children are remarkably active sleepers). Apart from this, there is nothing for you to do, except remain on call in case a minor crisis, like a nightmare, should occur (see Chapter 9, Some Common Problems).

Toddlers and Young Children (Evenings)

Information Sheet

Child's name and nickname or family name

Child's age

Tea

Time

Room (dining room/kitchen/sitting room in front of television)

Food

Drink

Place at table

Tablecloth

Plastic mats etc.

Bib, pinafore, napkin etc.

Feeder cup, special bowl, pusher etc.

Floorcloth

Degree of independence (self-feeding/partly self-feeding etc.)

Playing and television

Play area/room

Overalls, pinafore etc.

Newspaper (for protecting carpets, tables etc.)

Water/paste pots

Scissors

Favourite games

Television programmes and times

Toilets and potties

Toilet/potty trained (fully/partly/not)

Potty (where it is kept)

Child's word(s) for toilet/potty

Time 'lifted' at night

Degree of independence (pull chain/supervise clothing etc.)

Bathtime

Time

Heater

Alone/shared bath

Towels

Flannel

Sponge

Soap

Bath bubbles

Toothbrush

Toothpaste

Bath toys

Brush and comb

Bedtime

Time

Bedroom

Heater

Hot water bottle

Nightclothes

Dressing gown, slippers etc.

Bedtime drink

Prayers/story/game etc.

Favourite story

Cuddly toy/teddy bear etc.

Special instructions (glass of water/lamp on/door ajar etc.)

Other notes

Clean clothes (in case of accidents)

Personality (e.g. shyness, jealousy etc.)

7
Toddlers and Young Children – Daytime

Caring for young children during the day demands more of a babysitter in terms of energy, effort, imagination and attention than any other occasion. The children are old enough to be interested in everything and seem to have bottomless reserves of energy, but they are still too young to fall back on their own resources for entertainment for very long. In practical terms this is the most vulnerable time in their lives, for they are not yet old enough to recognize the dangers of some very tempting activities, such as playing with matches, and their spontaneous and wholehearted enthusiasm makes them oblivious to all kinds of hazards. The babysitter's task is the difficult one of maintaining careful supervision and anticipating potential catastrophe, without unwarranted interference and restriction of the child's fun and sense of wonder. Many of the topics covered in the previous chapter are relevant to daytime care.

Taking children out (Parents' notes)

This is the occasion when your careful selection of just the right person for the job really pays off (see Part One). Going out with a different adult on his own is an exciting adventure for a child. If you have confidence in your babysitter's ability to cope, it can be a rewarding one for everybody.

Providing adequate information about each of the children is your main responsibility. You must also make sure that the babysitter provides details of what she is planning to do. Try to allow five or ten minutes beforehand to run through the plan. Make a note of where she is going to take the children, how they are going to get there, how long she proposes to stay, whether they are going to do anything else, such as going to a restaurant or café for lunch, and what time she expects to be back. Also, if your babysitter is going to drive the children, make a note of what type of car she has, its colour and the registration number. A check-list for this information is included at the end of this chapter. These precautions are unlikely to be required in practice but they are worth taking.

It is a wise precaution to provide your children with some form of identification. When young children are lost, the distress is often so great that they are unable to answer any questions and they may not remember details such as telephone numbers. A plastic tag attached to a coat pocket is an excellent way of providing such information, but a label fastened with a safety pin serves the same purpose. A guide for this identification is included at the end of this chapter.

If your babysitter will have to pay fares or entrance fees or, perhaps, buy a meal or ice-cream, provide her with sufficient cash to cover the cost. Finally, give her a door key, even if you expect to be back before she returns. You might be delayed or she might return earlier than she planned.

Taking children out (Babysitter's notes)

Taking children out, especially for lengthy outings, such as an entire afternoon, can be very exhausting. The younger the children, the more tiring it is. Planning alone can demand the patience and skill of a battle commander. Nevertheless, if you have planned the outing properly, then you can all enjoy yourselves.

It is important to follow the plan that you have agreed with the parents. This does not have to be a tight timetable, but you can cause considerable anxiety if you are not where you are expected to be at the right time.

Travelling

Safety is a major consideration when you are taking young children out. They have little understanding of traffic and certainly cannot judge the speed of an oncoming car. Also, an excited child, seeing something interesting on the other side of the road, is quite likely to run straight to it without looking, unless you prevent him. Reins are the safest way of keeping hold of a lively toddler.

If you are not using reins, and some parents consider them unnecessarily restrictive, then you must hold the child's hand firmly all the time you are walking along the street. If you are in charge of one child only, keep him on the inside of the pavement, away from the road. If there is more than one child, hold the hands of the youngest. Games like counting the number of steps to the corner or spotting houses with green gates, are quite all right when you are walking along the pavement, although you should always have one eye on the children. When you are actually crossing roads, stop all games and concentrate on the business in hand. You can resume the game on the other side. Never dash across the road; always wait, however long, until it is safe to cross without hurrying. Wherever possible, use subways and pedestrian crossings.

Other danger areas are bus stops and station platforms and getting on and off buses and trains. Keep well back from kerbs and the edges of platforms and do not allow the children to run about and chase each other. Try to keep them occupied by telling them a story or playing a quiet game like 'I spy'. Hold hands securely when getting on and off buses and trains and always keep small fingers well clear of slamming or sliding doors.

While children are too small to use an ordinary adult seat belt, they must never sit in the front seat of a car. Special fitted safety seats are clearly best for very young children, but, of course, you are unlikely to have these in your car unless you have such children yourself. Confine young children to the back of the car and lock all doors. Impress upon them that they are not to touch door or window handles and that they should sit down. Long journeys without the help of another adult, or at least an older child, to supervise the young ones are really not recommended. Even shorter journeys can be something of an effort.

Obviously, you must keep your eyes on the road and concentrate on driving. This makes keeping small children amused and occupied rather difficult. Singing is fairly undemanding, and a cassette of children's songs is even easier. Alternatively, the children can play a 'spotting' game, when they have to look out for such things as a church, a school, a blue car, a black dog, a bus stop and so on. A favourite toy is a good idea, but avoid small things which can get lost on the floor and anything pointed or breakable, which might inflict injury if you have to stop suddenly.

If squabbles erupt, as they may well do during competitive games, stop the car before attempting to sort them out. Arguing with a recalcitrant three-year-old while steering through heavy traffic is dangerous and pointless.

Ventilate the car by opening the windows in the front rather than in the back. If a child does feel car sick, it is best to stop and walk up and down in the fresh air for a few minutes until the queasiness passes.

Basic equipment

The things you need to take with you will vary depending on your destination and your means of transport. A tote bag with a shoulder strap and zip pockets is invaluable. It leaves your hands free to hang on to the children and provides a safe place for your purse and so on so that you need not be encumbered by a handbag. Base your list on the following suggestions:

1. Packet of paper handkerchiefs (invaluable for general mopping up, as well as for blowing noses)
2. Safety pins (useful in cases of lost buttons and broken elastic)
3. Two or three individual wrapped plasters
4. Plastic bag containing damp flannel or foil-wrapped, impregnated tissues (very useful after ice-cream)
5. Small towel (it is surprising how easily children find wet places to play; also useful in conjunction with item 4)
6. Packet of non-sticky sweets (a useful diversionary tactic and bribe; may also help with travel sickness)
7. Coins for telephone (in case of emergencies)
8. Paper bag for rubbish, sweet papers etc. (public litter bins are never where they are needed)
9. One small, light toy or game per child

For longer outings, add:

10. Spare pants for each child (in case of accidents)
11. Small plastic bottle of diluted fruit drink and paper cups (children are always thirsty at inconvenient moments; better for poor travellers than canned, fizzy drinks)

Toilets

Encourage children to go to the toilet before they leave home, even if they are only going out for an hour. On longer journeys, take the opportunities provided by stops at cafés, petrol stations and so on to let the children use the toilets.

Some children graduate from potty to toilet quite quickly but others continue to use a potty for a relatively long time. If a child is not used to an adult toilet, then you will have to take the potty in a plastic bag.

Eating out

Eating out need not be a problem. Many restaurants and cafés serve child-size portions, although even these may be too big for small appetites. Avoid the more luxurious and elegant restaurants. Children tend to like places that are colourful and which serve such favourites as hamburgers, chips and milk shakes.

On each child's information sheet there will be details of his preferences for food to enable you to order easily. It is not a good idea to confuse a child by offering a choice of several different things. It is much better if you make up his mind for him. Rarely is any purpose served by trying to force a child to eat something he does not want. There is even less point if you are all on an outing intended to be a special treat. By all means, encourage a child to eat up his meal, but if he really does not like something, let him leave it. Do keep an eye on the choice of food and avoid too many mixtures and fizzy drinks, especially for children prone to travel sickness.

Where to go

There are many places to take children of this age-group. Outdoor activities are often best because they give the children a chance to let off steam. Trips to the park, where children can play on swings and slides in an adventure playground and kick a football about, are always welcome and often more popular than more elaborate outings. Many swimming pools have special areas for young children, protected from the main pool and under close supervision. The zoo is endlessly fascinating and some have a special children's corner. Museums are a bit advanced for this age-group, but exhibits of dinosaurs and other prehistoric animals are the exception and almost always capture the imagination. The cinema is a great standby and there are dozens of films suitable for this age-group. There are often special juvenile programmes at holiday times and some cinemas specialize in cartoons.

There are, of course, many other places to take children. Remember, however, that their span of attention is not very long and they can become bored quite easily. Also, their legs are small and long journeys are tiring. The secret of a successful outing is to keep it simple and make it fun.

Staying in (Parents' notes)

Leaving young children at home in someone else's charge is relatively straightforward. Adequate information about each child is, as always, essential. Do not forget to include instructions about meals, if relevant, and drinks.

Staying in (Babysitter's notes)

Much of the advice given in the previous chapter (Chapter 6, Toddlers and Young Children — Evenings) is applicable here. Arrangements for meals and using the toilet or potty do not change whatever the time of day and you will find the information on playing and television helpful.

Games and activities

Your main concern during the day is keeping the children happily and safely occupied. Young children have lively minds and lively bodies and they like to keep both active.

This is the age-group that most enjoys playing at 'grown-ups'. 'Shops' is a great favourite and requires little preparation. A selection of ordinary household items, such as a packet of tea and a tube of toothpaste, can provide the stock and a table makes an adequate counter. A cardboard box can be transformed into a cash register and you and the children can make price labels. You will almost certainly have to play the role of the customer and will, therefore, need a handful of small coins. Other games of 'grown-ups' include hospitals where dolls can be bandaged, playschool where teddy bears can be educated and, of course, the perennial favourite of mothers and fathers.

Most children are well supplied with toys and can spend quite a long time inventing complex games and making up lengthy stories with model cars, train sets, dolls' houses, toy forts and so on. Make sure that each child is happily occupied and not interfering with the others' games and leave them to it. There is no need to feel that you are shirking your responsibilities if you do not join in. Children will often regard your participation as interference and will resent it.

It is a constant source of surprise to adults that a child with a box full of expensive toys and games can still claim to be bored and to have nothing to do. At such times, it is useful to be able to introduce a new activity. Finger painting rarely fails to amuse. Provide large sheets of plain paper and thickly mixed paint. Protect the child's clothes with a plastic pinafore or overalls and the table and floor with thick wads of newspaper. Potato printing has a similar charm.

A slightly less chaotic activity is for the children to draw outlines of each other or of parts of their bodies, like hands and feet, on long strips of paper. The back of an old roll of wallpaper is ideal for this. One child lies very still on the paper while you, or another child, draw round him with a thick crayon. He can then draw in and colour his face and clothes, finishing up with a life-size portrait.

Making a collage can be an individual or group activity and requires nothing more elaborate than some paste, torn paper, scraps of fabric, etc. You may need to sketch in an outline to start things off.

None of these activities is particularly original but individual children may not have done them before. A large part of their appeal lies in the fact that they are new to the child and do not involve ordinary games and toys. However, having succeeded with them once, you may find that they fail to please on another occasion. If you look after the same children more than once, make a note of which activity you introduced this time and have a new one up your sleeve for the next occasion.

Boisterous games of the 'cops and robbers' or 'cowboys and Indians' variety are best played in the garden. These always involve a lot of shouting and running around and a fair amount of rough and tumble. You should keep an eye on what is going on, in case the game becomes too realistic and someone is hurt.

In the summer time, do not overlook the possibilities of a paddling pool in the garden. Fill it with slightly warm water and dress the children in swimming costumes. Do not leave the children alone with the pool because of the safety aspect, but keep clear of the splashing. If the children do not have an inflatable pool, different size plastic bowls and buckets are a good substitute.

For obvious reasons, most television programmes for this age-group are shown in the afternoon. Make a note of the time they begin (see Chapter 6, Toddlers and Young Children — Evenings).

Afternoon sleep

Some children, up to the age of four of five, have an afternoon sleep. If a child normally does so and is clearly feeling tired, take him up to bed and simply tuck him in comfortably. Draw the curtains to prevent the daylight from keeping him awake. There is no need for any special arrangements, such as storytelling, before an afternoon sleep. If the child does not wake naturally at the end of the usual period, wake him up yourself, perhaps with a glass of milk or fruit juice. He will probably be completely refreshed after his snooze and bursting with energy. Unless there is a particular reason, for example he feels unwell, do not leave him in bed, however sleepy he may be, because he will not want to go back to bed in the evening and this will upset his usual routine.

As children grow older, they lose the habit of an afternoon sleep. If a four- or five-year-old, who normally has a sleep, does not want to go to bed in the afternoon, do not force him to do so. If he is not tired, he will not be able to sleep and will only feel resentful. Instead, encourage him to do something quiet and restful, or you could read him a story.

Questions

Young children are full of questions and can plague you constantly with 'why?', 'how?', 'where?' and 'what?' Obviously, questions and answers are an important part of learning and you should endeavour to answer them. If you do not know the answer, say so honestly and suggest that you look it up in a book or that the child asks his parents when they come home. It is really very unhelpful and unkind to brush a question aside because you are busy or simply cannot be bothered. Whatever the subject, keep the answer simple and straightforward. Do not resort to saying, 'It is because I say so.'

Sometimes a child does not understand the nature of the question he is asking and this can make it difficult to answer. Many adults have been defeated by a dialogue on the following lines.

'What is it?'

'A squirrel.'

'Why?'

You must decide whether the child is genuinely interested in finding out about the squirrel, or whatever is being discussed, and has simply phrased his question rather curiously, or whether he is asking pointless questions because he is bored. If he is just bored, divert his attention from the interesting game of pestering you into something more constructive. This is also a sensible ploy when a child launches himself into a meaningless litany of questions, not listening to your answers and responding with yet more questions.

Helping

As well as playing 'grown-ups', young children like to do grown-up things and actually enjoy helping. By all means, encourage them to help you wash-up or lay the table. Select the tasks you give them. For example, they can certainly dry up saucepans, spoons and plastic mugs but should not be entrusted with sharp implements or breakable utensils.

Toddlers and Young Children (Daytime)
Babysitter's Information

Babysitter's full name

Car, colour and registration number

Other means of transport (bus/train etc.)

Destination

Timetable – Depart: Arrive:
          Depart: Arrive home:

Any other plans (meal/other visits etc.)

Rough outline of route

Toddlers and Young Children (Daytime) *Identity Information*

Date

Child's full name

Age

Address

Telephone number

Mother's name and telephone number

Father's name and telephone number

Babysitter's name

Babysitter's car and registration number

Toddlers and Young Children (Daytime) *Information Sheet*

Child's name and nickname or family name

_____

Child's age

_____

Outings

Whether travel sick (always/sometimes etc.)

Meal times

Suggested foods

Suggested drinks

Reins

Meals

Time

Room (dining room/kitchen/sitting room in front of television)

Food

Drink

Place at table

Tablecloth

Plastic mats etc.

Bib, pinafore, napkin etc.

Feeder cup, special bowl, pusher etc.

Floorcloth

Degree of independence (self-feeding/partly self-feeding etc.)

Toilets and potties   (See Toddlers and Young Children — Evenings)

Games and activities

Play area/room

Overalls, pinafore etc.

Newspaper (for protecting carpets, tables etc.)

Water/paste pots

Scissors

Paddling pool

Favourite games

Television programmes and times

Afternoon sleep

Time

Room

How long

Other notes

Clean clothes (in case of accidents)

Brush and comb

Swimming costume

No-go areas in the garden

Personality (e.g. shyness, jealousy etc.)

8
Older Children

Older children can safely be left on their own for short periods during the day. They can even be left in charge of a younger brother or sister and usually respond well to the responsibility, enjoying the sense of self-importance. However, after a couple of hours they can grow extremely bored and this may lead to trouble, either through lack of attention or deliberate mischief. Therefore, for prolonged periods during the day and if parents are going out in the evening, a babysitter is still necessary.

Parents' notes

Parents should supply adequate information about each of their children, but, of course, less detail is necessary than in the case of younger children. Without being too solemn, make it clear to the children that they are expected to pay attention to the sitter and to do as they are told.

Babysitter's notes

On leaving infant school, children undergo an amazing spurt of growing up. It is as if, once they have acquired the basic skills, from reading to tying shoe laces, they have become independent. They are constantly 'trying out their wings'.

The secret of successful babysitting with this age-group is to treat them as grown-ups and appeal to this independent side of them. The older the child, the better his response to this will be. Starting off with this attitude helps to avoid any confrontation with a resentful ten-year-old, who considers the mere idea of a babysitter an insult.

This does not mean that this age-group is necessarily troublesome or resentful. The children are, in fact, still at an age when they respond almost automatically to adults in 'authority', whether teachers or babysitters. Rebellion is an occasional thing and is much more likely to be directed against the parents than against someone outside the immediate family circle.

Meals

Parents will provide details about the times of meals and the menus on the information sheet.

There is no reason why children should not help you prepare a meal or lay the table. The younger end of this age-range especially, likes to be bossy and enjoys telling you what to do and, apparently, reversing roles and looking after you. Older children may be less willing to help, depending on the normal family routine.

Expect children to be punctual for meals, giving them fifteen minutes warning so that they can finish whatever they are doing. You can also reasonably expect good table manners. This does not mean, however, that a meal should be a solemn occasion. Encourage the children to talk about whatever seems to be interesting them, whether it is a forthcoming holiday or the problems of making a model plane. Do not fall into that most boring adult habit of asking children what they do at school and whether they like it. Generally, once school is over for the day, week or term, children have absolutely no desire to think about it.

Television and games

One of the advantages of this age-group's independence is that there is no need for you to supervise their activities, although it is sensible to know what is going on and where. Most children have hobbies which they happily pursue on their own. However, you may well be co-opted for board games and similar activities, especially by an only child. Do not cheat to let the child win. He will nearly always detect this and it will outrage his sense of fair play. Moreover, if he has played the game before, he is quite likely to beat you without your subterfuge.

If parents normally limit the amount of time a child may spend watching television or forbid certain programmes, this will be recorded on their information sheets. It is a good idea, in any case, for you and the children to decide together what programmes you will watch and then to stick to the plan you have made. Make a note of the times and remind the children a few minutes before their favourite programmes are due to begin. Switch off when the planned programmes have finished, otherwise the children are quite capable of sitting in front of the set until close-down.

Baths

There is no need for you to bath an older child and, indeed, he or she would resent this bitterly. About this time, both boys and girls develop a self-consciousness about their bodies and are appalled by the idea of a stranger seeing them naked. You should respect their feelings and not blunder into the bathroom unless it is really essential.

Getting the bath ready and cleaning it afterwards are quite different matters. You should see to switching on the bathroom heater, if necessary, running the water, putting out towels and nightclothes and so on. Leave him to wash himself and call out or knock loudly on the door when it is time to get dry and dressed. If washing the child's hair is on the agenda, do this yourself before he gets into the bath.

You can check that younger children have washed and dried themselves properly and make sure that teeth are cleaned before bed. In some families, children are taught to empty the bath and wipe round it from the time they are old enough to bath alone. In others, it is left to mother.

Children should not lock themselves in the bathroom or in any other room, for that matter. If you do hear the bolt slide across or the key turn, suggest that the door is unlocked immediately and reassure the child that you have no intention of intruding. Times when you may need to investigate are likely to be few and a word of warning through the door will probably be sufficient to speed things up or to stop over-enthusiastic splashing.

Bedtime

Turn on bedroom heaters and fill hot water bottles, if these are necessary, about thirty minutes before bedtime. Never use boiling water for hot water bottles in any case, and make sure that they are not so hot they will burn the feet.

If the child does not bath in the evening, give him fifteen minutes warning before bedtime. Make any bedtime drinks before sending him into the bathroom to wash his hands and face and to clean his teeth.

Older children will almost certainly be able to put themselves to bed. Many like to read for a little while before going to sleep. Check that a suitable light is switched on and, if a 'lights out' time is not specified, allow about thirty minutes for reading. When the time is up, be quite firm about closing the book, tucking the child in and switching the light off. Discourage the child from leaving a radio playing when he is supposed to be going to sleep. Preferably, remove both book and radio from beside the bed to the other side of the room. Many children of this age-group think kissing is 'sissy', so, unless he clearly indicates that he wants a goodnight kiss, do not give him one.

Older children are the ones most likely to get up to mischief when they are supposed to be asleep and those who share a bedroom may well encourage each other to be naughty. If you hear voices and giggling when the children have supposedly settled down for the night, do not rush into instant action. Wait for about ten minutes to see if they continue. A failure to provoke you may well take the spice out of the game. Too hasty action may encourage them to continue as soon as you have left the bedroom. If you do need to put a stop to giggling and games after bedtime, be firm and business-like without being bossy and cross and try not to lose your temper (see Chapter 9, Some Common Problems).

Taking children out (Parents' notes)

Provide adequate details about each child and ask your babysitter for details of the planned outing. If she will be driving the children, keep a note of the make, colour and registration number of the car.

Taking children out (Babysitter's notes)

Taking older children out presents few problems. Safety, while always an important consideration, is not the major concern as it is with younger children. Your main duty is to deal with the practical arrangements, such as buying cinema tickets, to make sure that you all get wherever you are going and to exercise a little control over high spirits. Once again, you will find that treating the children as if they are adults will be amply rewarded.

Travelling

Most older children are at least used to walking to school on their own. Some may even travel by bus or train each day. They have, therefore, learned to be fairly responsible about traffic and at stations. Little supervision is required, although, if you are looking after several children, you should round up stragglers from time to time. Also, make all the children wait together before crossing roads, going through ticket barriers and so on. You can expect reasonable behaviour on buses and trains and a noisy child will usually respond well if you point out that he is being a nuisance to other passengers. Children should not occupy seats on buses and trains while adults stand.

If you are driving, put the youngest children in the back of the car and allow the eldest to sit beside you. He should wear a seat belt. Older children can entertain themselves on car journeys but firmly discourage any games which involve hanging out of windows or jumping up and down. If you do need to suggest activities, you could try spotting specific makes of cars, or registration numbers in alphabetical order or counting the legs on pub signs in numerical order.

Eating out

Children have a great weakness for 'junk' food, so one of the chains that sells hamburgers and other fast foods is likely to be a good choice. Let the children select their own meals and do not worry if, for once, all the vitamins and proteins are not carefully balanced. This is an outing, so you should all be enjoying yourselves. However, it is not unreasonable to expect passable table manners. Do not let the merriment get so out of hand that it annoys other customers.

Picnics appeal tremendously to this age-group and need not be elaborate. Provide each child with an individually wrapped pack of sandwiches, an apple and a small bar of chocolate. Do not forget yourself.

Where to go

Local outings to places like the park are usually simple enough for an older child to manage on his own or with friends. An outing with you is rather more special and something of a treat. Exhibitions which tie in with a child's hobbies are always popular and these days museums, far from being dry and fusty places, are often packed with enough buttons to push and handles to turn to delight any child. Swimming pools are fine for an active afternoon and crazy golf is splendid for the less energetic. The cinema is a great standby and films and cartoons for this age-group are prolific during the school holidays.

Older Children *Babysitter's Information*

Babysitter's full name

Car, colour and registration number

Other means of transport (bus/train etc.)

Destination

Timetable – Depart: Arrive:
             Depart: Arrive home:

Any other plans (meal/other visits etc.)

Rough outline of route

Older Children *Information Sheet*

Child's name and nickname or family name

Child's age

Meals

Time

Room (dining room/kitchen/sitting room in front of television)

Food

Drink

Place at table

Routine tasks (laying the table/washing-up/drying-up etc.)

Television

Television programmes and times

Limited viewing

Banned programmes

Bath

Time

Towels

Soap

Bath bubbles

Shampoo

Toothbrush/toothpaste

Routine tasks (running water/cleaning bath etc.)

Bedtime

Time

Room

Heater

Hot water bottle

Nightclothes

Bedtime drink

'Lights out' (i.e. time allowed for reading etc. after going to bed)

Special instructions (curtains partly open/glass of water etc.)

Outings

Whether travel sick (always/sometimes etc.)

Meal times

Suggested foods

PART THREE

9

Some Common Problems

Ninety per cent of babysitting is trouble free, but a minor crisis can occur. Remember that all these problems are minor, although not necessarily trivial, and should be treated as such. Do not let any interruption upset you so much that you lose your temper or are reduced to tears.

Nightmares

Nightmares can be terrifying whatever your age and are especially frightening for young children who do not really understand what has happened.

If a child wakes up crying or screaming because of a bad dream, you must take his fears seriously. Go straight to him and switch on a lamp. Sit on the bed and cuddle him because physical comfort is essential. Do not try to stop him crying immediately as this is a good way for him to release his fears and tensions. When he is a little calmer, talk to him about his dream. If you can persuade him to tell you what frightened him, this will help you to calm his fears. Listen patiently and try to reassure him that there are no monsters or whatever. Do not ridicule his fears and avoid remarks like 'a big boy like you should not be frightened of the dark'.

When he has calmed down, begin to settle him back into bed. Stay with him until he is very sleepy or actually asleep. Leaving a light on often helps. If the child seems very apprehensive about going back to sleep, read him a story or chat quietly about something pleasant, such as a holiday or a pet. In extreme cases, let the child get up and sit with you. Wrap him in a dressing gown and make him a warm drink. Half an hour in a lighted room with you will reassure even the most timid child.

Quarrels and squabbles

Only children in films behave angelically towards each other. In real life, brothers and sisters quarrel quite often. Disagreements can be triggered off by all kinds of things from jealousy to one child accidentally damaging another's painting. Do not leap to your feet the minute you hear raised voices but, if the quarrel continues or looks as if it might turn into a full-scale battle, then put a stop to it. By far the best tactic for ending quarrels is to offer a diversion to one or both children. A new toy or a different activity is a great peacemaker. Do not make the mistake of taking sides and never blame an older child just because you feel 'he should know better'.

Discipline

You are unlikely to encounter any real problems of discipline. Children of all ages tend to reserve their bad behaviour exclusively for their parents and are usually quite tractable with people outside the immediate family circle. However, avoid confrontations wherever possible. Expect the children to abide by your rules but keep these to a minimum and make sure they are sensible.

Children can be naughty in a number of different ways, including angry refusal to co-operate, deliberate disobedience, tantrums and what the army calls dumb insolence. How you react and deal with these obviously depends on the age of the child and the seriousness of the crime. In all cases, try to avoid losing your temper.

When a child commits a minor misdemeanour a quick 'telling off' is usually sufficient. Make it clear that you will not put up with such behaviour and then dismiss the incident from your mind. Once again, an alternative activity is a good diversionary tactic. If the child commits exactly the same offence again, then you must be much more severe in what you say and, perhaps, impose a punishment, such as missing a favourite television programme.

With serious offences, you must make it very clear that the child has done something extremely naughty. Exert your full authority and make the 'telling off' solemn and memorable.

Take the child into another room and make him stand in front of you while you speak to him. Tell him at length what you think of his behaviour but remain calm throughout. If it makes him cry, so much the better. When you have finished, forget the incident and do not keep returning to it.

Sometimes the best way to deal with naughtiness is to ignore it. This is the most appropriate treatment for dumb insolence, tantrums and those occasions when a child thinks his tiresome behaviour is actually funny. If you are clearly unimpressed, then he will probably grow bored and stop. Avoid any desire to laugh, as this will only encourage him.

Sometimes it is helpful to point out how unhappy and disappointed mummy and daddy will be when they come home and hear what he has done. Never suggest to a young child that his parents will stop loving him because he has been naughty. He will believe you and, although it may stop his mischief, it will cause him immense distress.

Smacking children is a very contentious issue and libraries of books have been written about it. However, you will be wise not to smack. If the parents disapprove of this form of punishment, you will probably upset them. If they smack naughty children themselves, then the child will probably be unimpressed by such a punishment from you. You fail in both cases.

However, if a child provokes you so much that you do smack him, do not agonize about it afterwards. It will not cause lifelong psychological scars. In fact, he will probably forget about it before you do. One word of warning — the traditional 'clip round the ear' can actually damage the delicate hearing mechanism. If you are going to smack, aim for the bottom or thighs, where it will sting but do no permanent damage.

Persistent crying

A continually crying baby can be very worrying. When a baby wakes up and cries, first try the obvious solutions, such as changing his nappy feeding him or playing with him for a short while (see Chapter 5, Young Babies). Talk to him or even sing to him until he becomes tired or until he actually falls asleep. The cradle has gone out of fashion, but babies still like to be rocked. This is a gentle soothing motion and almost hypnotizes some babies into silence.

Teething can be a wretched, painful business and it makes some babies very irritable. The information sheet (see Chapter 5, Young Babies) will tell you if he is teething and any remedies his mother uses.

It may surprise some older babysitters to know that wind is a most unlikely reason for crying . Unless he has swallowed enormous quantities of air because his bottle was held at the wrong angle, a baby is unlikely to be suffering from wind. If he is, when you pick him up to cuddle him, he will bring the wind up. There is no point in spending half the night rubbing his back or tummy, and you will only make him more fractious if he wants to get back to sleep.

Recent research has shown that the younger a person is the more he dreams and babies dream most of all. It seems reasonable to assume that, if they dream, they may also have nightmares. A crying baby may simply be upset by a bad dream and want a reassuring cuddle.

If you have tried everything and the baby is still crying, then give up. Sometimes babies just work themselves up into a frenzy of crying. The more tired they are, the more they cry, making themselves yet more tired. All you can do is shut the door and leave them to it.

Refusal to eat

A child's refusal to eat, whether just one item on the menu or the whole meal, is not really a problem at all from your point of view. His eating, or non-eating, habits may be a headache for his parents but should not cause you anxiety.

Of course, you should use your common sense. A child who wants to lunch entirely on ice-cream should not be permitted to do so. He can have some ice-cream when he has eaten some of the first course. However, a child who decides he does not like Brussels sprouts will not instantly develop scurvy if he does not eat them. Nor will he die of starvation or malnutrition if he misses a meal completely.

You should begin a meal with the assumption that everybody is going to eat all of everything. Children have likes and dislikes and sometimes a former favourite suddenly becomes very unpopular. Do not let the matter become an issue or a battle of wills. Be calm and matter of fact about any refusals of food and do not try to force a child to eat something he does not want. There is no point to the prolonged misery of making a child sit in front of a bowl of congealing custard, forbidden to move until he has eaten it. He will not eat and he will eventually have to move.

This does not mean that you should allow children to do anything they like. If a child claims that he is not hungry or that he does not like anything on the table, then it is his choice if he wants to go without. However, if thirty minutes later he expects to fill himself up with crisps and chocolate bars, he should be stopped. It is just unfortunate if he has changed his mind and decided that he is hungry after all.

Reassurance

Children, especially young ones, are often shy with strangers and sometimes secretly worry that, when their parents go out, they will never return. When you are going to look after a child for the first time, you should arrange to meet him beforehand. This is very important, and if the parents do not suggest it, raise the idea yourself.

If a child is worried, reassure him by explaining his parents' absence in terms that he will understand. Compare a visit to the theatre to a trip to the Christmas pantomime and an evening spent with friends can legitimately be thought of as a party. Explain that his parents will return while the child is asleep. Sometimes, painting a picture for their return or making some other sort of 'welcome home present' provides tangible reassurance.

10

Safety and First Aid

Accidents can and do happen. Children seem to have a unique ability to find the most dangerous places to play and the most injurious things to play with. Nevertheless, by taking a few precautions, you can at least minimize the risk. Minor falls, cuts and grazes may still occur, but you should be able to prevent major injury.

If you are in any doubt about the child's condition following an accident, you should contact the family doctor for advice.

Telephone the parents if a child in your care seems ill, in pain or is vomiting for no particular reason.

Safety rules

1. Keep cigarettes and matches or lighters out of reach.
2. Do not allow children to play in the kitchen, unless secure in a playpen or highchair.
3. Empty aspirins and other tablets and pills out of your handbag before babysitting.
4. Do not leave babies alone with a bottle or anywhere they can roll off or fall.
5. Help toddlers up and downstairs and close the safety gate, if there is one.
6. Do not let children play on staircases.
7. Do not let children play near water, even a garden pond, alone.
8. Do not let children treat kitchen equipment or adult tools as toys.
9. Do not let children touch plugs or other electrical apparatus.
10. Keep to safety precautions introduced by the parents.

What to do in case of accidents

Cuts and grazes

Wash small cuts and grazes with plenty of clean water and pat dry with tissues. Apply antiseptic cream and an adhesive plaster if the child is young or to stop the bleeding. If a scab has already formed before the child shows you an injury, leave it alone.

Deep or gaping wounds should be seen by a doctor. Cover with a clean dressing but do not attempt to clean the wound or apply antiseptic cream. Take the child along to the nearest casualty department.

Cuts and wounds caused by garden implements, nails and similar things can cause tetanus. If you are in any doubt about recent tetanus immunization, take the child to the nearest casualty department.

Bright red, spurting blood indicates a cut artery. Immediately apply pressure with your thumb or finger just above the wound to stop the spurting. Apply a firm dressing and take the child to the nearest casualty department. Call an ambulance, if necessary. Do not apply a tourniquet.

Burns and scalds

Burns or scalds larger than about 3 cm (1 in) should be seen by a doctor. However, minor burns and scalds can be treated at home.

For small burns and scalds, immerse the damaged part in cold water immediately or hold under running cold water. Do not cover if there are no blisters. If there are blisters, cover with a clean, dry dressing. Do not prick the blisters or apply any creams or liquids. You may give junior aspirin to relieve the pain. Follow the manufacturer's instructions for the recommended dosage.

For serious burns and scalds, immerse the damaged part in cold water immediately. Cover with a clean, dry dressing and take the child to the nearest casualty department.

If a child's clothes catch fire, roll him in a rug or blanket to extinguish the flames. When the flames are out, wrap him in a clean sheet. Do not try to remove his clothes. Call an ambulance immediately.

Burns are always frightening. It is important to reassure the child to reduce physical and emotional shock.

Chemical burns

Wash the affected skin with plenty of cold water to remove all traces of the chemical. Treat as for burns (above).

Falls

Children fall over with remarkable frequency and more often than not cause little damage to themselves. If they do turn pale and cry, this is usually because they are skaken rather than hurt. A cuddle and kiss will comfort the child and this is very often all that is required.

If a child bumps his head, you should look for certain danger signs. These are vomiting, cuts on the scalp, extreme and persistent pallor, bleeding from nose, mouth or ears and loss of consciousness, even for a few minutes, during the following 24 hours. If a child goes to sleep after banging his head, check that his breathing is not laboured and, if you are at all doubtful whether he is asleep or unconscious, try to wake him. If you cannot wake him, this is a danger sign. If any of these danger signs are present, or if you are worried, telephone the child's doctor. He will call to see the child and may arrange for him to attend the hospital for an X-ray and/or observation.

A large swelling, especially on the forehead, can result from a bang on the head. This is caused by bleeding under the skin and, although sore and rather alarming in appearance, is not serious and does not require treatment. Of course, if it is accompanied by any of the above danger signs, then you should call the doctor.

Remember to tell the child's parents if he has banged his head so that they continue to watch for the danger signs until the 24 hours are up.

Fractures, especially in children are difficult to diagnose. Children's bones tend to crack on one side only, rather than break cleanly and this is not immediately apparent. However, if an injured limb continues to hurt, or it is painful to lift or put weight on, the bone may be fractured. If you suspect a fracture, take the child to the nearest casualty department.

Another type of fracture is less common in children and more obvious. The skin is penetrated and the bone is in direct contact with the air and at risk from infection. Immobilize the limb and take the child to the nearest casualty department. If a leg is broken, bandage it to the other leg. If an arm is broken, put it in a sling. Do not apply splints and do not give the child aspirin or a drink, in case he needs an anaesthetic.

Poisoning

If you find a child playing with household cleaners or medicines, assume the worst. Remove the source of poison and any tablets still in the child's mouth. If he is old enough to understand or another child is present, ask how many tablets or berries or whatever he has eaten.

Unless you are absolutely certain that he is not in danger, call an ambulance and while you are waiting, make the child sick unless he has swallowed:

oil paints

petrol products — petrol, paraffin, liquid polish, lighter fuel, dry cleaning fluid

insect spray

strong acids — carbolic, creosote, sulphuric, nitric, hydrochloric

strong alkalis — ammonia, bleach, washing soda, caustic soda

Put the child over your knee, face downwards, with a bowl to catch the vomit. Gently put your finger near the back of his throat and wiggle it about until he vomits. Alternatively, dissolve one tablespoon of salt in a tumbler of warm water and make him drink it. When he has vomited, give him a second glass of salt water.

If he has swallowed any of the poisons listed above, do not make him vomit. Give him a glass of milk to soothe the throat and to dilute the poison.

Take the poison container to the hospital with you to help the doctor. If you do not know what the child has swallowed, take a sample of the vomit.

Immediate treatment is essential, so do not delay getting the child to hospital.

Animal bites

Treat small bites as grazes (see above). Tell the child's parents so that they can arrange for tetanus immunization if necessary.

If the wound is very deep or the child is badly mauled, cover it with a clean dressing and take him to the nearest casualty department.

If a snake bite has caused swelling and pain, wash it in clean water and take the child to the nearest casualty department. Do not suck the bite or try any other home remedies.

Insect stings

Most insect stings are not serious. Cover with a cold compress or dab with calamine lotion to relieve the irritation. If you can see a bee or wasp sting and it is simple to remove, do so using tweezers. Otherwise, leave it alone.

If the area surrounding the sting becomes very inflamed, take the child to the nearest casualty department. If a child is stung on the tongue or inside the mouth, take him to the nearest casualty department.

Electric shock, drowning, suffocation
— the kiss of life

If a child has received an electric shock, switch off the appliance at the socket before touching him.

In the case of drowning, remove the child from the water immediately.

In the case of suffocation, remove the plastic bag or other cause immediately.

If the child has stopped breathing, give the kiss of life immediately. Do not stop to carry him indoors or to another room. Seconds are vital. If the child is still breathing by himself, however faintly, do not give the kiss of life.

Lay the child on his back and sweep a finger around his mouth to clear any obstruction. Tilt his head right back and support it with one hand. Press the chin forward with your other hand to open his mouth and to ensure that his tongue is not blocking his windpipe.

Pinch the child's nostrils together with your fingers, using either hand. Take a deep breath and cover the child's mouth completely with your mouth. Blow gently, watching to see if the chest expands. If it does not or if the stomach expands, arch the child's neck more and pull his jaw further forward.

Remove your mouth as the child exhales and breathe normally yourself. Give the first six breaths in quick succession and then continue at a steady rate of one breath every six seconds.

Continue until the child starts breathing on his own. This may be almost immediately or it may take some considerable time. While the skin remains pinkish in colour, there is a chance of recovery. However exhausting, persevere.

As soon as the child is breathing on his own, cover him with a blanket and telephone for an ambulance. Watch him closely in case he stops breathing and requires the kiss of life again.

Lay the child on his back

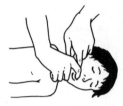

Clear his mouth of obstructions

Tilt his head back and support it with your hand

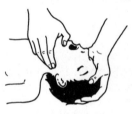

Press his chin forward to open his mouth

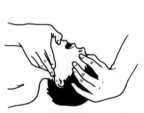

Pinch his nostrils together with your fingers

Cover his mouth with your mouth and blow gently

Do not leave the child while you are giving him the kiss of life, even to telephone for an ambulance. If you can, send another child to telephone a neighbour or call for help. Otherwise, drag the child you are resuscitating gradually towards the telephone or somewhere where you can call for help without stopping the kiss of life.

Objects in the eye

If the object is sharp or cannot be removed, take the child to the nearest casualty department.

Otherwise, gently lower the eyelid with the finger. If this does not remove it, irrigate the eye with castor oil so that the object floats out.

Objects in the nose and ears

If the object does not fall out easily, do not probe with tweezers or cotton wool. If it is wedged and is forming a solid obstruction, take the child to the nearest casualty department.

Nosebleeds

Some children suffer from inexplicable nosebleeds at certain times in their lives and, of course, these can also result from a minor accident. They are not serious and always look much worse than they are.

Usually they stop of their own accord and there is little you can do to help. It is best to sit the child down quietly with a handkerchief or other cloth held to his nose to mop up the blood. Otherwise, tilt his head back and place a cold, damp flannel across the bridge of his nose. Keys dropped down the back and other old wives' remedies are of no use.

A note on medical assistance

It is always wise to seek medical aid if you are in doubt about a child's condition after an accident. It is better to 'bother' a doctor unnecessarily than to let a child suffer, or even die, because you do not want to be a nuisance.

If you want advice about whether or not to take a child to a hospital, telephone the family doctor. Casualty departments are open 24 hours a day. If you are worried about a possible fracture, for example, take the child in your own car, in a mini cab or ask a neighbour to help.

In an emergency, dial 999. Ask for the ambulance service. State clearly your name and the child's address. Explain briefly what has happened.

If you do need to take a child to hospital, remember to take the Emergencies information sheet with you. Leave a note for the parents in a conspicuous place and telephone them as soon as possible.

Emergencies
Information Sheet

Doctor's address and telephone number

Local police station telephone number

Nearest hospital with casualty department (full address)

Ambulance service: dial 999

Name and telephone number of friend/neighbour to call on in emergency

Nearest telephone (neighbour/call box)

Parents' whereabouts including telephone number

Taxi and/or mini cab service telephone number(s)

Child's full name

Date of birth

Religion

Allergies (if known, especially to drugs and antibiotics)

Blood group

Last tetanus immunization

Parent or guardian (full name and address)